THE
COMPLETE SHOT

THE
COMPLETE SHOT
A practical guide for the field sportsman

James Douglas

Illustrations by Alan Hayman

BLANDFORD

For my wife Shena, my friend and partner, who has made so much possible
and my daughters, Morven and Isla, and my sons, Doran and Lyle,
who all in their way make my life so much richer.

A BLANDFORD BOOK

First published in the UK 1991
by Blandford
A Cassell Imprint
Villiers House
41/47 Strand
LONDON
WC2N 5JE

This paperback edition 1994

Distributed in the United States
by Sterling Publishing Co., Inc.
387 Park Avenue South, New York, NY 10016-8810

Distributed in Australia
by Capricorn Link (Australia) Pty Ltd
2/13 Carrington Road, Castle Hill, NSW 2154

British Library Cataloguing in Publication Data
A Catalogue record for this book
is available from The British Library

ISBN 0 7137 2503 6

Typeset by MS Filmsetting Limited, Frome, Somerset

Printed and bound in Hong Kong by Colocraft Ltd

Contents

Introduction

Field sports have changed a great deal as developments in social attitudes have altered the public's perception of them. Fifty years ago all field sports were accepted as part of our national heritage, as another country pastime that devotees enjoyed. Today it is different. People have become much more conscious of field sports and of the great damage done to some of our more exotic wild creatures by our sporting forefathers. However, field sportsmen also often take the blame for situations which have arisen from a wide variety of other reasons — greater demands made on the land, the clearance of wilderness areas and unscrupulous trade in the skins of some and the ivories of others.

It is unfair that the modern field sportsman should be held responsible for the excesses of his forefathers. It makes as much sense as the British not forgiving the Italians for using us as gladiators, or black Americans disliking us because we once shipped slaves. It is, however, the modern sportsman's responsibility to act, and to be seen to act, with respect for his quarry, the environment and for all wild creatures, that he should conduct both himself and the sport in the correct manner and, of course, always strive to improve his understanding and knowledge of the game. Responsible game shooting is vital to the future of both our wildlife and wild places. It is in our hands that the long-term success of our wildlife lies.

With international travel so freely available to anyone, we have in many ways reached a new and second age of the British travelling abroad to shoot. Whether you wish to shoot wild sheep in Mongolia, duck in Mexico or deer in Russia, it is now a simple matter of booking, paying and going. However, the real bulk of field sportsmen wish to enjoy their sport on a regular basis within easy travelling distance of their home. Wonderful rich sport is to be found throughout the British countryside if you know how and where to find it.

Shooting is also of huge economic importance to Britain's economy. Large numbers of people are employed by it throughout the country, either directly or indirectly, whether it be the gamekeeper whose association is obvious or the seamstress working in a factory making waxed jackets. However, the future of field sports is not assured. It is constantly under threat from both the well-meaning and the ignorant, and must constantly be defended. Our best method of defence is knowledge, the knowledge that comes from practical experience coupled with the written word.

EDITORIAL NOTE

Converting metric measurements to Imperial.

Throughout this book measurements are usually given in metric. Those readers who are more familiar with Imperial might find the following useful.

To convert cm to in: × 0.39
(to convert in to cm): × 2.5

To convert m to ft: × 3.28

To convert m to yards: × 1.09

To convert km to miles: × 0.62

To convert hectares to acres: × 2.47

To convert sq. cm to sq. in: × 0.15

To convert g to oz: × 0.035

To convert g to lb: × 0.0022

To convert kg to lb: × 2.2

CHAPTER ONE

Shotguns

TYPES OF SHOTGUN

Most people take up shooting after being introduced to the sport by a friend and much depends on the area you live in whether your first influence will be clay or game. Obviously someone who lives in a country area, surrounded by an abundance of rabbits which he is free to shoot, is more likely to be game orientated than an individual who has game denied to him and whose nearest shooting facilities are a clay pigeon club.

Whichever your first inclination or your introduction to the sport may be, there will come a day when you will buy your first gun. Walking in to a gunshop can be a daunting experience — great wall displays of guns in varying calibres, some over-and-unders, others side-by-sides, some sidelocks, some boxlocks, all gleaming attractively, and a salesman, not always as knowledgeable as he should be, eager to relieve you of your cash.

Shotguns come in many forms and different price ranges, from the cheap and crude through the inexpensive and useful to the fabulously expensive work of art. Simply put, they all do the same job, but depending on a variety of factors — weight, balance, size — some do it better than others.

The governing factor in the purchase of your shotgun, no matter what variety you eventually choose, is what you can afford. It is, however, good advice when buying a gun to look around, to try several, to consider buying second-hand and to buy the best gun your pocket will stretch to. It will pay dividends in its use and is more likely to last longer and retain its value, for whilst two guns of differing prices may look similar, it is the quality of manufacture that you are paying for: the fit of wood to metal, the tolerances of the working parts within the action and of course the quality and configuration of the walnut of the stock. The chequering on a good gun is crisp and artistic and done by hand – the chequering on a cheap one is machined and looks it.

Unless you are a very competent shot, I would recommend a visit to a good shooting school where you can try both over-and-under and side-by-side under the eye and guidance of an experienced shooting instructor, for it is he who is most able to identify your individual peculiarities – body size, arm length, your fluidity in movement and which is your master eye. He will also enquire what type of shooting you wish to do – one of the variety of clay disciplines, driven game, rough shooting, or a combination of all. Take his advice, he is the professional. He will be able to recommend a gun of a specific weight and length with which you will perform best. Whether you use an over-and-under or side-by-side is partly a matter of choice, though some people will shoot better with one or the other.

What is of great importance when choosing a new gun is fit. The best guns are made to fit the individual's body size, making his gun a natural extension of himself. Cheaper guns come in a wide variety of sizes, and like buying clothes off the peg, it is a case of getting the one that fits you best. It is an experienced job fitting a gun to an individual, and when buying a new gun, it is advisable either to know the measurements you require or to go to a shop that is equipped to measure you.

Over-and-unders have vastly increased in popularity in Britain over the last few years. An over-and-under is simply a gun which has the barrels arranged vertically, the principal advantage of this configuration being that the action can be built around the barrels, giving a more secure fit than the side-by-side. However, since more metal is used in the construction of the over-and-under action, and it necessitates an additional rib running along the top of the barrel, the over-and-under is a heavier gun than a similar side-by-side. To load an over-and-under the gun must be opened much further to allow the bottom barrel to clear the action so that the cartridges can be dropped in. Nor does the over-and-under enjoy the same aesthetic appeal as the side-by-side, since with its deep profile many people find that it looks clumsy and inelegant.

The enormous rise in popularity of the over-and-under, how-ever, can be attributed to several factors. The first is directly linked to the growth in clay pigeon shooting. Not only do more

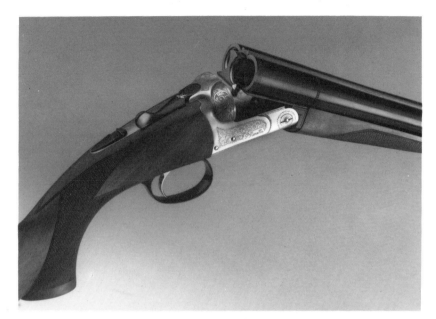

Beretta 626, side-by-side boxlock ejector. A typical good quality working boxlock with single trigger.

people find it initially easier to sight down a single barrel, rather than the slightly more confusing pair of a side-by-side, but the greater weight necessitated by the construction of the over-and-under means that it greatly reduces the recoil that your shoulder must absorb when firing. Moreover, with the fore-end wrapping up around the barrels, your hand has greater protection from hot metal when shooting a round of clays.

Most over-and-unders feature the single trigger mechanism, allowing you to select which barrel you wish to fire, the selector mechanism being controlled from a little switch incorporated in the safety and operated by your thumb. The advantage of a single trigger is that your gun hand remains in exactly the same position when firing your second barrel. The mechanism will either be of the spring system or utilize the inertia of the recoil of your first shot. It is for this reason that most over-and-unders incorporate a comfortable pistol grip, unlike the side-by-side which normally features a double trigger, necessitating a

Beretta 686 game gun, over-and-under boxlock ejector. This gun is the bottom of the range and consequently could be regarded as best value since it has all the technical qualities of the guns at the top of the boxlock range, but with little spent on embellishment.

Beretta 687 game over-and-under boxlock ejector. Better quality wood, hand-finished with game scene engraving.

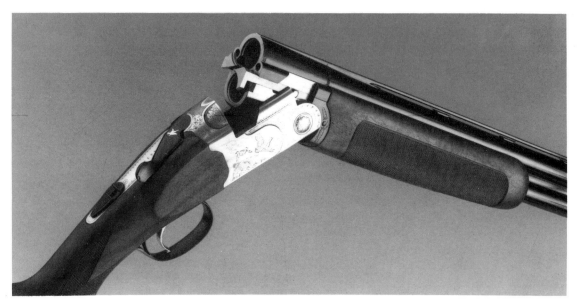

straighter hand grip so that the hand, on firing the first shot, can comfortably move backwards to reach the second trigger for the next shot. The consequence is that, with the increase in clay pigeon shooting, large numbers of sportsmen have become completely familiar with the handling and use of this style of gun, and when they have expanded their activities to include game shooting, they have demanded guns of the same configuration.

The other principal reasons for the dramatic increase in popularity of the over-and-under are price and availability. High-tech engineering in Italy and Japan, where most modern over-and-unders are made, has made available enormous numbers of these guns at prices which are highly competitive. The manufacturers, identifying the widely differing uses to which the guns are put — the varying disciplines of clay and game — and the differing financial brackets of the users, have developed a variety of guns to cater for both the sportsman's needs and the sportsman's financial status.

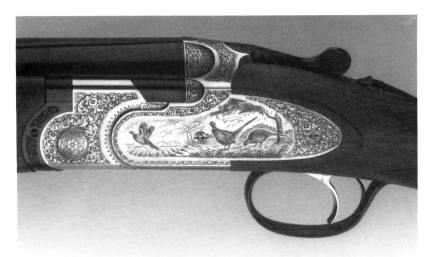

Beretta 687 EELL game, over-and-under, side-plated boxlock ejector. Top of the boxlock range, the mechanics are the same as the 686, but superb wood and hand-engraving over machine outline.

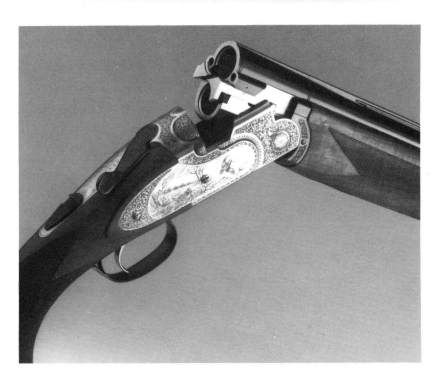

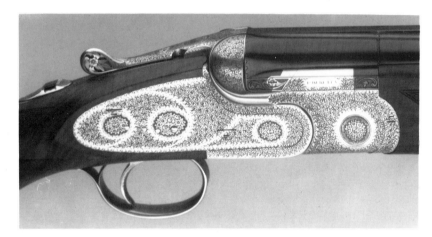

Beretta SO6 EELL. This is the Rolls-Royce of the Beretta over-and-under range. Hand-made from start to finish to any customer specification.

Probably the ultimate example of the gunmaker's art is the British side-by-side. When shooting was the sport of the very wealthy, the sportsman demanded and was prepared to pay for the best. Thus was financed the development of gunmaking to its finest form. However, the great gunmakers of England, and those few in Scotland, would never have developed had it not been for the enthusiasm that Queen Victoria had for Scotland, for it was she who created the fashion for the aristocracy to have houses in Scotland amongst their deer herds and grouse moors. At this time, game of England and abroad was also enjoyed by the Victorians.

The development of the sporting gun was carried out by the British gunmakers in their constant efforts to improve and refine their creation, to make the gun superior in its handling and performance for the game shooter. All unnecessary weight was trimmed away, the balance and fit were given great importance, and the result was a beautiful combination of elegant fit and design with minimal weight and enormous strength to ensure smooth working and safety with continual use.

Having created these magnificant guns, the gunmakers then developed and refined the embellishment on the outside. Engraving in its most complex and finely detailed form was offered as an additional decoration on the outside of the gun. Indeed, this also allowed the purchaser to have his gun made more individual by his choice of engraving. Such decorated guns today are phenomenally expensive and few individuals would ever be fortunate enough to own one. Those who do would do better to keep it pristine in a vault, since such a gun will appreciate in value like any other work of art.

The sidelock was a refinement added during the great period of development of the classic English gun. Simply, a sidelock consisted of two separate locks, one for each barrel, and was perceived to be less likely to let you down. Furthermore, if you were going off on your annual shooting holiday, it was a simple insurance to take with you two additional locks so that in the unlikely occurrence of your gun breaking down, your shooting holiday would go on uninterrupted.

The sidelock came to be regarded as an essential part of the best British guns, and as a result of this heritage arose the idea that a sidelock is superior to a boxlock, which does exactly the same job, the difference being that it has only one action contained within the box to serve both barrels. This superiority may have been the case during the heyday of the British manufacturers, but it does not follow with modern guns. Indeed, given a choice of an inexpensive sidelock or boxlock of comparable price, normally the boxlock nowadays would be the better buy. Nevertheless, socially they were perceived to be different in the past, the sidelock being associated with the more expensive gun.

Another feature which differentiates guns is whether they are of the ejector or non-ejector type. A non-ejector is a little cheaper, but it is well worth the money to pay the extra for an ejector. With a non-ejector, once you have fired the cartridge you have to open the gun and manually withdraw the spent cartridge, whereas the ejector, once fired, will throw out the spent cartridge allowing for speedy reloading. This facility is invaluable when shooting driven birds, or in any other situation where you wish to reload quickly.

One cautionary word, however — it is very wrong to throw your cartridges out and leave them. In a situation where you may be shooting driven birds, the cartridges would be collected after the drive. However, when you are shooting by yourself it is a simple matter to get used to opening your gun with your hand over the action so that the spent cartridge does not land on the ground. You can easily drop it in your pocket. If you do eject your cartridges on to the ground, you should pick them up and take them home with you. The brass is certainly not biodegradable, and there is nothing more objectionable than empty brightly coloured cartridges lying around the countryside.

Another consideration is the choking of your gun. The choke refers to the constriction at the end of the barrel, just before the muzzle. The degree of choke governs the tightness of your pattern of shot at range. The tightest choke, full choke, should hold 70 per cent of the pellets from your cartridge inside a 30 in (75 cm) circle at 40 yards (36 m). A true cylinder barrel is the opposite of full choke and has no choke at all. This would mean at the same range only 40 per cent of your pellets would be in a 30 in (75 cm) circle. Other choke measurements are quarter, half and three-quarter choke.

For game shooting it would be unwise to shoot a bird at close range with a full choke barrel, as the damage to the carcass would be likely to render it unsuitable for the table. For game shooting probably the best advisable combination is to have one barrel lightly choked, perhaps with a quarter choke, and the other with a three-quarter choke. There are many different varieties of choking. One exceptional shot I know favours a true cylinder on his left barrel and full choke on his right. This means that he can deal with close birds with his left barrel without causing undue damage to the carcass, whilst a bird further out will still be in a dense pattern of shot using his right barrel.

Many shotguns now offer the facility of variable chokes. These are small sleeves that you select and screw in to the barrel depending on the targets you are expecting to encounter. This gives enormous versatility to your gun.

It is of course advisable to check the patterning on your gun with the brand of cartridge and shot size you intend to use. Whilst it is a simple matter to do this on your own, because of the number of targets you may need to use it is better to go to a shooting school where they have this facility.

Patterning your gun is a simple matter. At the set ranges of 20, 30 and 40 yards (18, 27 and 36 m), you fire a cartridge at a white painted metal plate and count the density and even spread of your cartridge. Ideally you are looking for a uniformity of pattern. Experience will show you which cartridges are best suited to your gun, since it does not follow that a gun which patterns beautifully loaded with No. 6s of one brand of cartridge will shoot equally well with a different brand. Indeed, the cartridge can affect the pattern from a barrel almost as much as the choke. Old-style felt or composition wads or some of the new biodegradable wads will perform differently from a cartridge which is loaded with plastic cup wads, developed for clay shooting and designed to keep the lead shot together during its journey down the barrel. These plastic cup wads are not advised for game shooting since they have a tendency to concentrate the pattern much more and they are certainly not welcome additions to the countryside.

If you were patterning your gun yourself you would have to use white cardboard or plywood, and of course at close range it is difficult to count the pellet strikes, since often large holes appear where clusters have struck.

The most commonly used shotgun gauge for almost all clay shooters and most game is 12-bore, though 20-bores have become very popular, giving a performance comparable with the 12-bore. The cartridge, being smaller, contains less shot, but the 20-bore will allow you to shoot at ranges more or less the same as a 12-bore. The advantage of a 20-bore is that it is lighter on the shoulder.

The .410 is really only suitable for close range at small game and vermin, but is an ideal beginner's gun, particularly for youngsters taking up shooting. It allows the user to get acquainted with a real gun, to become familiar with the handling, the safety, manners and the etiquette of shooting, without suffering the punishing recoil that the larger gauges deliver.

It should, however, be understood that the bore of the gun has nothing to do with the range. It does not follow that a .410 is less powerful and achieves less range than a 12-bore, since the pellets from a .410 travel at the same velocity as those fired from a 12-bore. The only aspect in which they differ and which accounts for the greater range allowable with a 12-bore is that the 12-bore cartridge, being bigger, contains more pellets and so allows the shooter to shoot a denser pattern at greater range.

There are other sizes of shotgun — 10-bore, 8-bore, 4-bore — but the cartridges are extremely difficult to obtain. Most owners of these large calibres have to load their own. It should, however, be said that while they are of interest and certainly I would not refuse one as a gift, it would be as a curiosity. They have little practical use in today's shooting field — apart from the horrendous expense of a cartridge, it is quite literally using a sledge-hammer to crack a nut. These large calibres were developed as fowling pieces in an effort to reach further and kill more than one bird with one shot. But those days have gone, and whilst it is of intrinsic interest — and certainly good fun if you possess one to use it occasionally — for practical purposes they are no longer viable.

All guns sold in Britain must by law have been tested at an independent government proof-house. The same applies in Spain, France, Germany, Belgium, Austria and Italy. Under the strictest supervision each gun is fired in a captive chamber with a measured charge to ensure that the gun will withstand the highest pressure which a cartridge would deliver in the chamber of the gun. The gun is then proof stamped under the barrels, giving the chamber length and the mark of the proof house, either London or Birmingham. You should of course only ever use a cartridge of the length that the gun is chambered for, or less. Never be tempted to put a cartridge of greater length into your gun and fire it, otherwise disastrous results will occur.

Rust is the great destroyer of guns. It is no respecter of even the most expensive shotgun, and will attack with astounding speed if the gun is left wet or uncleaned. Irrespective of how tired you are at the end of the day, it is vital that before you minister to your own needs, you must thoroughly dry and clean your gun.

The procedure is simple. The outside of the gun should first be thoroughly dried. Next, the inside of the bores should first be scrubbed out with a phosphor-bronze wire brush and cleaning solvent, then dried with cloth patches until they come out clean. Oil on the wool mop should then be lightly applied on the inside of the bore. There is little point in putting great amounts of oil into the barrels — it doesn't offer any more protection and excess oil drains down the barrel when the gun is stored, through the action and into the stock. Finally wipe the outside of the gun with an oily cloth and inspect the whole gun — stock, barrels and fore-end — to ensure that it is completely moisture-free, before storing it in your gun cupboard.

CARTRIDGES

Shotgun cartridges are as diverse as the opinions of the users regarding the benefits of the many brands. There are cartridges to accommodate every species that you might ever shoot, from the collection of small birds for scientific specimens (dust shot), to

wild boar (Brenica slug), and they come in a variety of prices and attractive packaging.

A superb example of a large forest-dwelling European stag.

Following the simplest human instincts, most people will assume that keeping to a cartridge and shot size with which they have succeeded is preferable to changing both brand and size, whilst others who perform badly in the shooting field can fall into the trap of blaming the cartridge.

It should be understood that greater power, i.e. magnums or any of the higher and more powerful cartridges, will not necessarily perform particularly well in your gun. What is of first importance is that you pattern your gun as I have previously described and that you should use a cartridge recommended for the quarry species you intend to shoot. It will not enhance either your accuracy or bag to use a more powerful cartridge with a larger shot size. Indeed the opposite may well be the result.

A good example of this is the cartridge that some insist is the secret of success for geese. I know people who maintain that BBs are the perfect choice, stating that with the size of a BB you need only have one or two in a vital area to bring the bird down. Such a statement is both inaccurate and unsporting. A BB does not give the density of pattern at range that a smaller shot size would deliver. The idea that one or two pellets in a vital area is all that is required is against all sporting ethics. It does not account for the possibility that several pellets could equally easily lodge in a non-vital area, allowing the injured bird to fly on carrying pellets only to suffer and die at a later stage.

It is therefore an important decision that you must make and it should be made carefully when choosing the cartridge. A good guide is the following table:

Quarry	Shot size
Snipe	7 or 8
Pigeon, grouse, teal, partridge, woodcock, squirrel	6 or 7
Pheasant, rabbit	5 or 6
Mallard, widgeon	4, 5 or 6
Hare	4 or 5
Geese	1 or 3
Fox	1 or BBs
Boar	Brenica slug

It would, however, be unnecessary and silly for you to carry with you a variety of shot sizes. You will discover that for game shooting throughout the season, one shot size will account for almost everything you shoot. This shot size will be either 5, 6 or 7. These sizes will more than adequately deal with all sporting quarries, with the exception of geese, that you will find in the UK. A more selective shot size can be chosen for specific quarry. If you had booked a goose shooting holiday, for instance, then you would take with you a quantity of 1s, which you would only buy specifically for geese or foxes.

SHOTGUN SAFETY

Safety in the field is the most important consideration of the day. All shooters should school themselves in the actions of safety so that it becomes second nature and at all times you are seen to act responsibly and with safety in mind. It is not acceptable practice EVER to have your gun closed in company, even when you know that it is empty. When walking from peg to peg, guns should always be broken. The ONLY time a gun may ever be closed and loaded whilst you are walking about should be when walking up birds or rough shooting, and even then you must learn to think 'safety'.

The first and most elementary safety factor is the correct method of closing your gun, yet probably this simple action accounts for the most common fault amongst most shooters. The correct way to open your gun is with the gun pointing at the ground; break it open, using your thumb on the top lever and allowing the barrels to fall forward. Load the gun by placing the cartridges in the breach, then holding the fore-end in your left hand, lift the stock up with your right, closing the gun, maintaining the barrels' position pointing to the ground. When you have fired the gun, again break the gun and remove the spent cartridges, repeating the manoeuvre. This action is one of those simple operations that once practised becomes second nature. It is totally forbidden by good safety practice, even when you are on your own, to lift the barrels to close the gun.

When crossing fences, ditches or any obstacle which requires more than a simple step, if you are in company, you must always open your gun. If for any reason, whilst in company, you wish to carry your gun closed, or lay it down closed, you should open the gun and say to your companions, whilst presenting them with the open breach, 'Will you please note my gun is empty'. If you say this slightly formally, it will give your shooting companions the clear indication that you take shooting safety seriously. This is important: everyone should endeavour to be regarded by their companions as being exceptionally safety conscious.

It is totally unacceptable in company to walk about, say from drive to drive, with your gun closed. It is equally unacceptable to allow another to do it, irrespective of his social standing, and if you saw a fellow gun with his gun closed it is important that you quietly ask him if he would mind opening his gun. Alternatively, ask the host or shoot captain to have a word. But do not, for fear of either upsetting someone or not being invited back, compromise.

I had a good example of this at a formal shoot I was attending as a guest. Whilst walking from drive to drive I noticed that two elderly gentlemen were walking with their guns closed. They were chatting away to each other amiably with their guns under their arms, pointing at the legs of the fellow in front and his dog. When we stopped I noticed that one of them had his gun pointing at the midriff of another. I quietly and politely asked him if he would mind opening his gun. He was outraged and insulted, but I persisted until he opened his gun, which indeed was empty. Later that day, in the same circumstances, I again asked the fellow to open his gun, which was empty. He felt sufficiently insulted to complain to the host about me. Fortunately the host took my side.

A few weeks after this incident the same two elderly gentlemen, who were obviously shooting companions, were walking from one drive to another when one slipped and fell. His gun went off and badly peppered an unfortunate labrador. It could easily have been the labrador's owner.

Shooting from a hide is another situation in which safety must be rigidly enforced. It is the one situation where it is permissible, under strictly laid down rules, to put your loaded and closed gun down. If you are sharing a hide, it is of vital importance that you decide in advance who will shoot, rather than two or more people trying for the same bird. If you are shooting from a hide

The sportsman's normal view of a woodcock as it dashes away.

which is made of 'camo' net you must never leave your loaded gun leaning against the net. Nets are unstable and likely at any time either to collapse or catch in your clothing as you move.

An example of when it is permissible to put your gun down when shooting from a hide is when shooting geese. Hides are invariably cramped and it can be extemely awkward to break your gun to load it and then turn it round so that it is pointing upwards, since when sitting in a hide the only acceptable position for your gun is pointing straight at the sky.

Hides are often against fences or walls; if so, be sure that you put your gun where it cannot possibly be knocked over, i.e. threaded under one of the wires and firmly against the fence post. This will allow you a little more comfort in the cold cramped conditions you are likely to encounter – only pick your gun up when birds are about. The reason you might keep it loaded rather than load it when you are ready is that, apart from keeping it pointing skywards as I have described, movement within the hide is kept to a minimum.

If you intend to have a dog in your hide, the dog should be properly trained, and its position should be as far as possible from the gun, where it should lie quietly until it is required. If your dog is not fully trained, adult and reliable, it is unwise to take it into a hide where you have a gun, loaded or unloaded. Guns are easily damaged, and putting your empty gun down anywhere in the vicinity of a dog that is not totally reliable is asking for it to be knocked over.

SHOOTING TECHNIQUE

The man who could come up with an instant answer as to why people miss and who could prescribe some magical cure that would allow the sportsman to hit everything he shot at would be a very wealthy man indeed. Unfortunately, shooting would quickly become extremely boring if sportsmen needed only to point their guns and pull the trigger, for it is the degree of uncertainty every shot has which makes that very challenge so exciting. Every bird is different. We do miss some, so the feeling of achievement on taking a good shot is part of the attraction of the sport.

However, missing, whilst acceptable on occasions, is not the object of the exercise. All of us strive to be better shots and an understanding of the simple mechanics of shooting can greatly enhance our accuracy and appreciation of the sport.

As I have previously said, the fit of the gun is of great importance and the best possible way of learning to shoot is to go to a good shooting school where the instructor will teach you the correct stance and swing and be more likely to prevent you developing bad habits. However, most people tend to be taught by friends, picking up the rudiments, and with a little trial and error can muddle through with varying degrees of success. Yet an understanding of the basics of shooting can be of help to everyone.

The correct mental attitude, physical stance and swing are what we must learn. Let's take rough shooting. Part of the great attraction of rough shooting is the uncertainty, working cover, normally with a dog, in search of either a bolting rabbit or of flushing out a bird. What is important is that you take your time. It is never necessary to jerk your gun up like a sharp shooter. There is always plenty of time to identify the species of flushed game, lift your gun, swing through and shoot. We must be aware of the position of others and of course of our dogs at all times. It is the greatest temptation for newcomers to the sport to become so engrossed with excitement and so intent on the game that they are unaware of where they are swinging their guns.

Whilst it is important to take your time, what you must not do is consciously aim. Nothing is more guaranteed to make you miss. I have been in hides shooting geese on several occasions with individuals who are international clay shots and one would therefore assume that any bird they lifted their gun at would be in the bag. Yet when you see birds coming towards you from a long way out, with plenty of time to study them, the error the inexperienced make is mounting their gun too soon. The very anticipation and preparation for the shot seems to guarantee a miss and the secret of success in such a situation is to keep your gun down, mounting it in one fluid motion when the bird is almost overhead.

The same applies in a driven situation. A bird viewed well out in front and tracked as though you were handling a rifle is almost certainly going to fly on unscathed. Keep your gun down, keep your eye on the bird and when it is almost overhead lift, swing and fire. The idea is to shoot the bird when it is still just slightly in front of you, so that if you were to take a second shot, because you missed on the first, your second shot should be almost as the bird was directly overhead.

I am frequently asked how far ahead one should swing. This question is particularly common with regard to larger quarry such as geese, and several myths have evolved about shooting such birds. An example of the sort of silly advice that is constantly preached is that you shoot a gate's length in front of the bird. There is no way that anyone could possibly say how far ahead one should swing, since each bird is likely to be travelling at a different speed and will be at varying ranges. Add to this computation the length of your barrel and the chances of being able to state accurately how far ahead one should fire are negligible.

The only way to learn swing is to remember that, since every bird is likely to be travelling at a different speed and at a different range, you must concentrate on the bird's head as a target, and that you must lift your gun and swing through the bird. As your barrels pass through the bird's head, blanking out the bird, that is the moment to pull the trigger, still maintaining the smoothness of your swing. It is only experience that teaches your brain how quickly to swing and when to shoot.

Swing and fluidity are of course vital to the good shot. Like any other sporting activity, if you are going to swing you must have a firm base so that you can pivot from the waist without falling over. If mounting your gun when standing at a bird that is travelling away from you, you should keep both feet flat on the ground with your weight forward over your left leg. If the bird were coming towards you for an overhead shot, you would mount your gun in the same way, swinging through whilst pushing your left hip forward and lifting the heel of your right foot.

The technique of shooting from a hide, whether it is for geese or pigeons, is different from when either walking or standing at a peg. Shooting geese from a hide needs a little extra care. If you are sitting in a hide and geese are coming towards you, watch the birds through the net and remain motionless. Do not be tempted to pop your face over the top of the net for a better look. Keep in mind the simple motto — if you can see them, they can see you.

I know of a man many years ago who would have done well to remember that advice. Having shot and wounded a tiger, the beast vanished into the long grass. The gentleman in question, thinking he was being extremely clever, nipped up a tree to give himself a better view over the grass where the tiger had gone.

Too late he discovered that, whilst he could certainly see the tiger from this vantage point, it could also see him! He was fortunate to have had a guide with him who was also a good shot.

No matter how uncomfortable you are, keep still until the geese are almost overhead. Let them well inside your arc of fire, then picking an individual bird, mount your gun. If you are shooting alone, then the decision of whether you will shoot sitting or standing can be made at the last moment. However, if you are sharing the hide with a friend you must decide beforehand whether you intend to shoot sitting or standing. It is imperative that both of you do the same thing, otherwise the one who is standing up is in danger of being shot.

If you intend to shoot sitting then you will have built your hide at a height which allows you to shoot unrestricted. When shooting from a sitting position, keep the gun between your knees, with your eye on the bird through the net. The gun should have the stock resting on the ground. A good tip for muddy ground is to have a small rubber mat or piece of plastic to sit your gun on to keep it from becoming unnecessarily soiled. The barrel should be pointing straight upwards with your left hand on the fore-end. The gun should be mounted in one single movement and as the stock comes into your shoulder you should swing and fire.

Shooting from a standing position in a hide requires more co-ordination since in most instances you will start off from a sitting or crouched position and move into a stand before shooting. Calmness and fluidity of movement are even more important here. You must throw your gun up first as you begin to rise, your body following the gun in one fluid movement. It is an easy manoeuvre if you practise at home by squatting with your gun butt on the carpet, the gun held between your legs pointing at the ceiling. Mount your gun as you stand up, all in one simultaneous movement – the aim is that the gun should sit into your shoulder as your legs straighten, then you are free to swing. The reason that this manoeuvre should be practised is that when shooting from a hide, movement should be kept to a minimum, as from the moment you start to move it must be assumed that the bird has seen you.

Whilst you must take your time, you should not stand up and then mount the gun. Apart from the additional time this takes, you will discover that if you are holding your gun with the barrels pointing skywards, if you stand up prior to mounting the gun it will most likely end up pointing under your chin.

The goose shooter in his hide, dressed for the weather, holding his gun correctly.

Furthermore, if you were to hold the gun in the hide as you would normally, under your arm, then in the heat of the moment it's almost guaranteed that you will end up with your barrels being caught in the net.

The main reason for this quick mounting action is that geese have large and effective wings. When coming in with the wind in their faces the birds need only tilt their primary wing feathers and in the time it has taken you to stand up and mount your gun they are already out of range, rising vertically at great speed. How they achieve this is easy to demonstate. The next time you are in a moving car stick your arm out of the window, and using your hand as a blade, find how easy it is to make it aerodynamic as it cuts into the wind. Tilt it up or down and you will find your arm quite literally whipping away. Now imagine the effect on a goose with its two powerful wings.

The most common complaint I have heard from novice wildfowlers is that they heard the shot strike the bird and yet it miraculously flew on. This usually results in the sportsman seeking ever bigger, better and more powerful cartridges, which he erroneously thinks is the answer to his problem. Yet the answer is simple: he has not swung anywhere as well through the bird as he should and it is the leading edge of his pattern striking the trailing edge of the goose's wing or tail feathers that he has heard. It should be remembered that the shot string is 3 metres long. A few pellets from the front of the string striking the bird will probably prove to be ineffective. If you swing through the bird, catching it in the middle of the pattern, you should have no problem.

A shotgun's maximum *effective* range is 35 metres. Yet a substantial number of shooters seem unable to grasp this simple fact. Certainly it is true that a cartridge loaded with No. 5s and fired at an angle of 45 degrees will send the pellets over 250 metres. But we must keep in mind that the combination of pattern and velocity means that your effective range is only 35 metres. When you then consider that most game shot is within 12 to 20 metres, it puts into proper perspective the great silliness and cruelty of shooting at ranges which are obviously outside that which can be considered humane. Yet substantial numbers of shooters still maintain that for one or other reason, such as a particularly potent cartridge or tight choke, they can achieve kills at ranges of 55 metres and over. Whilst such feats are possible, the amount of game merely wounded is considerable.

What is always in question is the ability of the shooter to judge range, for whilst some have an almost uncanny knack of judging distance with considerable accuracy, many shooters seem unable to grasp how to judge it at all. The judgement of distance over familiar ground is relatively easy, and although you may be used to judging distances over a flat area like a playing field, your ability to gauge range over unfamiliar ground may be questionable.

Water is notoriously difficult, but so also are steep slopes, broken ground with rock, undergrowth, etc., and when you look into the sky, since there is no reference point unless there is a tree as a yardstick, it is very difficult to judge range, particularly when you add into the calculation the differing sizes of game. A snipe at 15 metres could look positively distant, especially in relation to a greylag goose, which would appear to the unfamiliar eye as though it were very close.

There are a few little tricks you can employ to help you learn how to judge range. If you are out walking, glance at a fixed point — a stone, a tree, a fencepost — and guess your judgement of its range. Then pace it out. If you are in a hide, lay out sticks or stones at paced distances in an arc around your hide so that you know exactly how far away they are. If you were to put them at a maximum range of 35 metres, you would know that when a bird was inside the arc it was within your effective range.

Another technique is to use the height of any surrounding trees. Bearing in mind that it is a rare tree in Britain that is taller than 20 metres, if you were to take the tallest tree in your area and imagine another sitting on top, this would be about 40 metres. This should help you judge the range of flying birds, and with a little practice the ability to compute the three factors of distance, speed and size will become instinctive.

CHAPTER TWO

Rifles

DEVELOPMENT OF THE RIFLE

The word 'rifle' is derived from the Old French verb 'rifler' meaning 'to scratch', and refers to the rifling or spiral grooves cut inside the barrel. If you were to take a bullet out of its cartridge and try to drop it down the barrel of a rifle of the same calibre, it would come as some surprise to discover that the bullet is in fact of slightly greater diameter than the bore of the rifle. The reason for the bullet being slightly oversized is that on firing the cartridge, as the bullet is forced down the rifle barrel, the rifling grips and cuts into it, compelling it to spin at a rate 150 times faster than an aircraft propeller.

As the bullet accelerates down the barrel, it spins at great speed and emerges from the muzzle in a stabilized state known as gyroscopic action. This means that the bullet with its high speed rotation will travel forward, giving maximum resistance to side wind pressure and keeping on an accurate line to the target. Without oversizing the round, the bullet would wobble about inside the barrel, would emerge spiralling and would not be very accurate, whilst without rifling, the bullet would fly out in an unreliable fashion and be completely ineffective beyond a short range.

The earliest form of rifling was called 'scratch rifling', but there is an apparently endless list of rifling designs – oval boring, gain twist, multi-groove, V-shape, ratchet, segmental, square groove, hexagonal. However, almost all modern rifles are now made by the most expensive but by far the best method, that of cold forging, also referred to as hammering or swaging.

The ultimate stalking rifle, a Holland & Holland with Mauser 98 action. Highly priced and quite beautiful.

Detail, showing the Holland & Holland quick detachable scope mounts.

The process is of course almost entirely automatic today, and starts with a bar of steel which is drilled through. The hole is then polished to a size slightly larger than its eventual rifle size. The rifling is ground into a separate tungsten carbide rod or mandrel of the exact size that the finished barrel is to be. The mandrel is then fitted into the barrel blank, and swaged, i.e. hammered onto the mandrel by a huge rotary hammering machine. By hammering the barrel on to the mandrel, perfectly accurate rifling is achieved whilst simultaneously hardening the steel, the action of compressing the molecules increasing the barrel's tensile strength. The resulting barrel will therefore be more accurate since it will have less whip or vibration under the impact of the cartridge explosion. It will also have a longer working life, since it will be more resistant to wear.

The choice of calibres and available models of the modern sporting rifle is extensive, with prices that range from the cheap to the expensive. However, rifles do not, even at the most expensive end of the market, cost anything like as much as shotguns. Apart from the obvious reason that rifles are cheaper to make, shotguns, since they are carried and seldom laid down, have evolved with much decoration, engraving and fine quality woods, whereas even the best rifles must be expected to withstand rougher treatment. This is particularly so in the northern hemisphere, where stalking invariably involves crawling through rocks and heather. Like shotguns, rifles are made by all the principal manufacturers, though the better ones generally come from Northern Europe – Germany, Austria, Sweden, Finland and Czechoslovakia. Sadly Britain no longer has a large rifle manufacturer, though superior rifles are still made in the UK at the more expensive end of the market.

Holland & Holland, better known as makers of fine English shotguns, are one such manufacturer. The company was founded in 1835 by Harris J. Holland, a well-known sportsman and pigeon shot of the day. In the 1870s he was joined by his nephew Henry and the first Holland & Holland factory was set up. At this time much of their effort was concentrated on rifle-making under the guidance of William Froome, the factory manager and a brilliant practitioner of rifle ballistics.

Holland & Holland continued as innovators across the whole field of rifle-making and by the 1920s had a list of about twelve proprietary calibres to their name. Their work included cartridge design and in 1904 they patented the first belted rimless cartridge, a refinement which guarantees accurate seating of the cartridge in the chamber and thus ensures regular striker blows and better ejection, irrespective of minor variations of diameter in cartridge case or chamber. As recently as 1989 Holland & Holland demonstrated their continuing ability with the introduction of the .700 Holland & Holland nitro express, the most powerful proprietary calibre in existence.

Methods of manufacture by Holland & Holland continue unchanged and rifles are hand-built to individual order. Since the introduction of breechloading in the mid-nineteenth century, Holland & Holland have built rifles on most actions but are best known for Mauser magazine rifles (still built on original 1898 actions). After the lull in the safari market in the late 1960s, double rifles are enjoying renewed sales, including an increasing number used for driven shooting in Europe.

Whilst there are many calibres available to the sportsman in the UK, many of them, it would be fair to say, are unnecessary and do much the same job. Some have slight benefits in being faster, slower or heavier, but nonetheless all the different calibres have their enthusiastic devotees. However, for all practical purposes for the game that you would expect to shoot in Britain with a rifle, four calibres would deal with everything – the .22

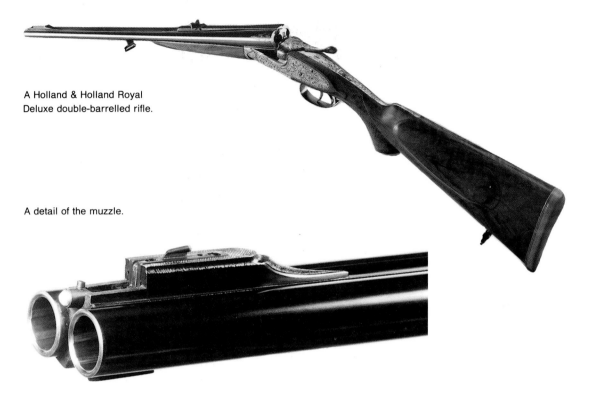

A Holland & Holland Royal
Deluxe double-barrelled rifle.

A detail of the muzzle.

rimfire for small game and vermin, the .243, the .270 or .30–06 for larger species such as foxes and deer.

If you could easily buy the various calibres without the long process of having to justify your choices to the police – and of course the expense of the weapons – then it would be ideal to have them all as they all have their different plus points. A good example is the .22 Hornet, a really good calibre with lots of punch, but what can you shoot with it? It is too loud and has an unnecessarily heavy punch to shoot rabbits. It certainly is an effective calibre for hares, but this advantage is cancelled out since there are few places in Britain where hares can safely be shot with such a rifle, and in any event the meat destruction is undesirable.

Some of the larger calibres have generally been designed for European, North American or African use. Whilst they are first class for this purpose and would adequately deal with our largest species of game – red deer – they tend to be impractical when applied to smaller species. Unless it is your intention to shoot big game outside the UK on a regular basis, it is difficult to justify the purchase of calibres specifically designed for your intended

Top An example of a good medium-priced rifle, the Sako Finnbear Hunter in .270W.

Above For the woodland stalker there is much to commend the shorter Stutsen stocked rifle. This example is a Sako Forester, with full stock in .243W.

quarry. Furthermore, there are many differing local calibre restrictions throughout Europe and you may find that what is allowable in one country may well not be in another. My advice to the British sportsman is to buy the rifle best suited to what he will most regularly wish to stalk – this calibre will more than adequately deal with the majority of game species. Should he ever wish to hunt in an area with calibre restrictions, then he can always hire the correct calibre locally.

TYPES OF RIFLE

There are four basic rifle types: bolt action, lever action, automatic and pump action. The bolt action rifle is regarded by many as the classic one for use in both military and sporting weapons. Simple in design, it really has never been bettered since the Mauser model of 1898 which is still in manufacture today. It is simplicity in that a magazine of cartridges is held below the action. By drawing the bolt back a cartridge is fed up into the action by spring pressure. Then by pushing the bolt forward, the cartridge is fed in to the chamber. The bolt is then locked down and the rifle is ready to fire.

The lever action rifle will be familiar to anyone who has ever seen a Western movie in which the hero has used a Winchester.

The trigger guard is part of a lever which, when pushed downwards, slides the bolt backwards whereby a cartridge emerges from the tube magazine under the barrel. By raising the lever the bolt is pushed forward, locking the cartridge in the chamber ready to fire.

The automatic rifle either uses the recoil or, more commonly, the gas produced by the firing of the previous round to blow back the slide bolt and feed a cartridge into the chamber ready for firing. This is the fastest way of reloading and is the same basic action employed by all machine weapons. It is the type used in most military rifles where a high rate of reload and fire is preferable to the lighter weight and more pinpoint accuracy achieved by a bolt action.

The pump or slide action rifle is similar to a lever action, the difference being that the cartridge is fed into the chamber, then ejected after firing by sliding the fore-end back and forth with the left hand.

The bolt action rifle is the strongest, safest and most accurate of the four basic rifle types. Not for nothing do the specialist long-distance shots (military snipers) use the bolt action rifle. It combines great versatility, light weight and freedom from mechanical problems and is the ideal choice world-wide for a stalking rifle.

The most important requirement from a rifle is for it to be consistently accurate — it must fire round after round in the tightest group possible. It may come as a surprise, but there are several points in the construction of a rifle which can cause it to give an unreliable performance. Enormous effort has gone into research by many manufacturers in the search and refinement of accuracy.

A rifle may be divided into a number of different parts. The barrel and action forms one piece, and a further piece is made up of the stock, which is simply a handle to which the rifle is fixed, allowing it to fit the user's body and be used with comfort. It is the fixing or fitting of the metal to the stock that is the first critical point at which accuracy can be compromised.

A rifle can be best understood if it is compared to a tuning fork. When struck by the explosion of the cartridge, the rifle vibrates throughout its length. If the joint with the stock is not very tight then the 'tuning fork' will not ring true. Due to tiny shifts in the metal and wood joint, the resonance of the metalwork will differ, and by not ringing true, the resonance of the barrel will vary from shot to shot microscopically. This minute variation in the bullet's flight is greatly magnified as the bullet travels several hundred metres, resulting in inconsistent accuracy.

Walnut is the favoured choice of wood to make the rifle stock as being close-grained it does not easily crack or warp and can be intricately worked with comparative ease. Walnut also has the advantage that it is both strong and lightweight. The quality of the wood used in a stock not only affects the performance but can of course also greatly enhance the perceived value of a rifle, particularly if it is good heart wood, with beautiful colour and grain. Some of the less expensive rifles use maple, particularly Canadian rock maple or beech, but neither of these woods has the natural figuring of walnut.

Recent developments in stock construction have all but done away with the compromise between durability and portability that wood represents, giving instead the guarantee that the rifle stock will be impervious to temperature changes and moisture and that it will always react exactly the same, time after time, thereby providing optimum performance. Unfortunately these modern materials — wood with composition laminates and polymers — do not have the natural beauty of wood and have less aesthetic appeal. They do, however, provide enormous strength and are incorporated into the more workmanlike models of most top manufacturers.

This is illustrated in the difference between one of my own rifles, a Steyr Mannlicher, and a friend's rifle, another Mannlicher.

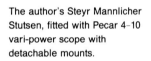

The author's Steyr Mannlicher Stutsen, fitted with Pecar 4–10 vari-power scope with detachable mounts.

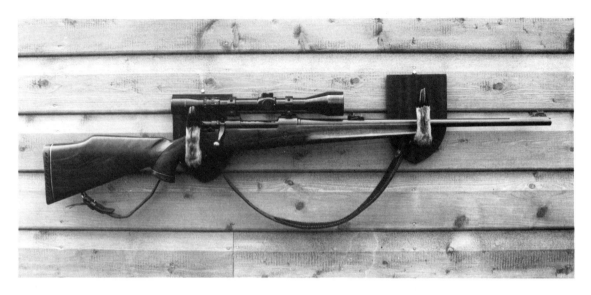

My rifle has a wooden Stutsen stock and is rather beautiful, but does require care and oiling, and because it is a natural material, it is liable to absorb moisture, particularly under adverse winter stalking conditions. My friend's rifle has a composition stock and whilst to my taste it has no aesthetic value whatever, it does the job wonderfully well — fitted with a bipod, something I would be reluctant to do with my rifle, he can attain exceptional accuracy. I suppose the difference is one of attitude. I tend to regard my rifle as an instrument, an object of beauty and a pleasure to use. My friend's attitude, on the other hand, is more practical. He regards his rifle as a tool which performs a task for him with great efficiency, aesthetics to him being of secondary importance.

The author's Parker-Hale fitted with Pecar 4–10 vari-power scope with detachable mounts. I have shot more deer with this rifle than most men will in a lifetime.

SIGHTING AND TELESCOPIC SIGHTS

Irrespective of the accuracy your rifle is capable of, if you cannot place a bullet confidently with accuracy in the target, then your rifle is ineffective.

There are three types of sight for the rifle: open, aperture and telescopic. Almost all rifles are fitted with open sights. These are the simplest sighting devices and take the form of a post or blade fixed on top of the barrel at the muzzle, which is lined up with a V or notch sight fixed at the other end of the barrel.

In my opinion it is important for the rifle user to learn to shoot with open sights before fitting a scope. You then have the confidence of knowing that, in the event of your scope being damaged or rendered inoperable due to bad weather, you can remove it and continue stalking rather than the alternative of at least a wasted day and perhaps a ruined holiday.

Aperture or peep sights utilize the post or blade sight at the muzzle, but have a small ring sight fixed on the action close to the eye.

The telescopic sight is by far the easiest to use and the most efficient. Unfortunately it is also more prone to damage. Because the telescopic sight has this drawback and can be rendered useless in driving rain or snow, most sporting rifles are fitted with both open sights and the facility to mount telescopic sights.

The telescopic sight comes in two different formats, fixed power and vari-power. The fixed format ranges from $3 \times$ magnification up to $6 \times$. Powers greater than $6 \times$ would not be advisable — whilst they provide greater magnification of the target, they equally provide greater magnification of any movement or vibration. I would recommend $4 \times$ as the best choice for most shooting conditions, giving excellent light enhancement while bringing the target to one quarter of the actual distance away. For this reason the $4 \times$ is the most commonly used.

Vari-power or zoom scopes come with several magnification capabilities, but the norm would be $4 \times - 10 \times$. Although I do have vari-power scopes, it should be understood that the greater magnification does not necessarily make taking the shot easier. Indeed, my own vari-power scopes are almost always set at $4 \times$. The occasions and conditions for which I increase the power are very rare indeed, and then I only turn it up to $6 \times$.

One of the reasons why I do not recommend vari-power is that it does not give you the opportunity to get used to the sight picture within your scope. By this I mean the fact that your eye will quickly become familiar with the size of a given species that you look at regularly. Experience in using your fixed power will act as an additional range guide.

This was illustrated on one occasion when I was stalking with a friend of mine who was an excellent shot at targets, but at the time had no experience of stalking. Indeed, this was one of his first outings. We came to a gorge and spotted a roebuck out on the hill beyond the other side of the gorge. It was a difficult situation to judge range, there being no reference points between ourselves and the deer. My friend was insistent that the buck was over 150 metres away, while I, having examined it in my scope, was convinced that the range was a maximum of 110 metres. We later proved he was out by slightly over 25 per cent, the range being accurately measured at 105 metres.

The other reason I do not recommend vari-power scopes for the novice is that there is a permanent temptation to turn up the power, to compensate for poor sighting conditions or longer range, unsafe shots. By constantly varying the power in your scope, you do not give yourself a chance to become totally familiar with your equipment, and it is familiarity with your own capabilities and with those of your equipment that separates the mediocre stalker from the excellent. By both studying ballistic charts and getting experience of firing your rifle at a target, you will learn naturally to consider range, windage and bullet drop, and make the necessary adjustments confidently and instinctively.

A good illustration of this was provided by the same friend I referred to earlier, some three years later after he had gained a great deal of experience stalking in a variety of conditions under my guidance. We had stalked a party of stags and shot one each at a range of some 70 metres. The sounds of our shots obviously disturbed any deer in the area and we both spotted a stag about 220 metres away, appearing from some dead ground. He was obviously wounded (not by us but probably from the neighbouring estate). Almost without hesitation, my friend lifted his rifle, tracked the wounded animal as it moved slowly away and fired, shooting it cleanly through the heart. He had automatically gauged bullet trajectory, windage and the animal's forward motion with pinpoint accuracy, something he could only have achieved with the total confidence in his abilities and familiarity with his equipment that experience had given.

Reticule

There are several styles of reticule (the cross inside the telescope) available in telescopic sights. Some of the more expensive scopes offer you the facility of changing the reticule, whilst others come with the style of reticule fixed. The choice of reticule is entirely a personal one. My personal preference is for a pre-plex which I find gives me the facility of being able to shoot with minimal delay in all light levels.

Scope mounts

Scope mounts vary. The simplest and least expensive is the screw clamp attachment, one of which is fitted to each end of the scope. They are attached to the rifle by a screw which draws two little jaws together similar to a vice into recessions cut into the top of the action to receive the mounts. This design can be most reliable. However, by far the best mounting system is the roll-off scope mount. Two permanently fitted receivers are attached to the top of the rifle with female joints. The scope is fitted with rings with male joints protruding from the bottom, engineered to great tolerance. Fitting your scope is simple: the front ring is fitted, then the scope is turned to locate the rear mount and locked into place. The roll-off mount, whilst being very much more expensive than the clamp variety, is infinitely preferable, particularly in situations which require the quick removal of your scope – heavy rain or snow – and it is guaranteed to fit perfectly back into place when required.

Zeroing open sights

Most open sights are designed so that the top of the blade or post is aligned with the top of the V in line with the target. Almost all rifles with open sights will have a variety of leaves, fold-up small metal plates, each one with a V and a range marked on it – 100, 200 and so on. Alternatively you may have a sliding V that you manually push up two pillars which have graduated ranges marked on them. It is a simple matter of practising with a target at different ranges, using the firing technique described on p. 43.

You should remember that your eye cannot focus on an object close to and on an object at a distance at the same time. One or other will go out of focus. Most people using open sights find that their eye will focus first on the rear sight. Then, as it places the blade in the V, focus naturally will go to the blade. In other words, most people find that the rear sight becomes a blur. Your eye will then focus on the target, perhaps 90 metres away. You will find your eye altering focus as it aligns all three – rear sight, blade and target. You will get used to this. As in all rifle shooting it is practice that is the key to achieving your optimum performance.

Using a peep or aperture sight requires the same basic technique as the open sight, the difference being that the tiny hole helps your eye to focus, rather like a camera, over a greater depth of field, your eye being automatically centred in the hole. However, light loss in such a tiny hole inevitably makes the target difficult to see clearly, particularly when there are low light levels.

Eagles rarely harry red deer. Alan painted this picture after we had witnessed this unusual site in Glen Lyon.

Zeroing the telescopic sight

Whether you have your scope mounted on a .22 or you are zeroing a scope mounted on a large-calibre rifle, the technique of zeroing is the same, only the ranges at which you shoot will differ. When zeroing a full bore rifle it is advisable to wear ear protection as the repeated explosions can damage your hearing. If you do not have ear protectors, then at least stuff your ears with cotton wool which will give some protection.

Unless you have access to an approved firing range, it will be necessary for you to find a safe area of countryside where there is a good bank or hillside into which you can fire. It is imperative that in choosing the area in which you are going to zero your rifle you ensure that you have the best possible place to shoot from a prone position. It is also of vital importance that there is no possibility whatsoever of your bullets ricocheting in any direction where they could endanger people or stock. Equally, you must ensure that your bullets cannot travel on, but will be contained within the bank at which you are shooting.

The first stage is to get your vertical reticule directly centred on your line of fire. Take a sheet of plain white paper on which you have drawn a 1 cm wide, 60 cm long vertical black line. Tape the paper to a heavy cardboard box. Then at a range for your .22 of no more than 10 metres and for a full bore of no more than 40 metres, fire a shot aimed at the centre of the line. At the range you are firing, you should see where the bullet has struck. Then adjust the vertical line on your reticule accordingly and repeat. When zeroing you must take your time and concentrate on every aspect of your position and breathing. Continue firing and moving your vertical line until you achieve three consecutive bullets striking the line.

Now replace the sheet of paper with another on which you have drawn a 1 cm wide cross. Position your target for your .22 at 50 metres, and for your full bore at 100 metres. Go to your firing position and carefully fire three shots, aimed at the centre of the cross. Go to the target and ensure that the three shots are on the vertical line. Now adjust your horizontal reticule, either up or down accordingly, to bring the point of impact of your rounds for the .22 on the centre of the cross. For your full bore you should aim to strike 2.5 cm high, the reason for this being that the bullet will be 2.5 cm low at 200 metres. (These figures are based on .243 100 gr. bullet, but you should check the ballistic tables for the calibre of your own rifle.) Since all the game you will be shooting with a full bore in normal stalking situations will be within a maximum 200 metre range, within that distance your bullet will be striking within 2.5 cm either below or above the centre point.

FIRING A RIFLE

There are several positions which you can take when firing a rifle – prone, sitting, standing. Whichever position you take you should understand that you're trying to make a stable tripod from which your rifle can be held rock steady. That tripod can be your elbows and chest if prone, your feet and buttocks if sitting, and in the case of standing, a bipod of your two legs.

Prone is the easiest position to fire from. Ideally you want to be lying behind a hummock, giving support and making your position generally more comfortable. However, invariably in stalking situations, the ground is not obliging and you will often be compelled to take a shot from a seemingly impossible position. It is therefore necessary that you practise prone shooting from flat ground as much as from ideal contours.

Lie with your legs open, preferably with your feet braced against rocks or the inside sole of your boot braced against the grass, to give you a feeling of stability. Get both elbows positioned as far apart as feels natural and comfortable, bringing the rifle into your shoulder. In this position you should be looking through the scope. Breathe naturally. If you have just gone through an exerting crawl and are out of breath, try to lie quietly and regulate your breathing. Unless the animal you have stalked is suspicious of your presence or moving, you are best advised to pause a few moments to collect your breath and composure. Slip off the safety with your thumb, and keeping your trigger finger off the trigger, hold your scope on the area that you intend to place the bullet – heart or base of neck. Breathe in and out. When you are ready gently depress the trigger on the point of breathing out. I believe that almost every stalker on the point of firing, probably momentarily holds his breath, but to recommend this could be misleading. You should not hold your breath but should practise gently squeezing the trigger as you are equally gently breathing out.

If, however, the circumstances demand that you take a faster shot than I have described, then you must judge whether you have the time and ability to take the shot with confidence. You must avoid taking a hurried shot, or one in which your accuracy could in any way be compromised. This inevitably results in misses or, worse, wounding.

Often when stalking, particularly in long grass, it is necessary

to raise yourself up above the level of the surrounding vegetation so that you can take an uninterrupted shot at the target.
When stalking down a steep slope, where it is impossible to take
a prone shot at an animal perhaps on a facing slope, it will be
necessary to take a sitting shot.

Sitting on your bottom, with your knees drawn up and feet
apart in a comfortable position, put your elbows on the inside of
your knees and raise the rifle to your shoulder. Brace your elbows
outward against your rigid legs. In this position you will find
after a little practice, that you can make highly accurate shots.
You may discover that in this position your lungs are slightly
constricted and your breathing not as free as in prone, but it isn't
a problem if you remain relaxed.

Inevitably when stalking, particularly in woodland, you will
find yourself in the position of having to take a shot whilst
standing. Obviously, if you have a handy tree or rock to support
yourself, so much the better, but it is seldom the case that such
support is to hand. Therefore practising a standing shot is a
necessary part of your preparation.

Many people advocate the use of a stick to provide support
when taking a standing shot. However, unless you are used to
walking with a stick, this simply means you have another piece of
equipment to think about, and I would advise you to get used to
achieving a high degree of accuracy without using a stick as an
aid.

Taking a standing shot is simply a case of standing with your
feet apart, three-quarters on to the target and regulating your
breathing, firing on exhalation. Once you have familiarized
yourself with taking a standing shot then practise taking a shot
from as many varied positions as you can imagine, perhaps on
one knee or with your legs apart. The idea is to keep the bottom
part of your body from the waist down as a locked firing
position, whilst your upper torso and shoulders should be able to
follow a target, swing or take a shot in whatever position you
find yourself.

You can practise at home with an empty rifle. Pick a mark on
the wall at eye level. Then holding your rifle, mount it to your
shoulder and bring the cross on to the mark. Hold on the target,
then put your rifle down. Repeat this in as many varied positions
as you can. The aim is to become completely familiar with the
handling of your weapon so that you can mount it smoothly at a
target which may be at an angle that is not ideal.

THE RIFLE CARTRIDGE

To understand how a rifle cartridge works consider how a blowpipe works: a projectile is fitted at one end of a tube and is then blasted down the tube on its journey to the target with a force of air.

There are two forms of rifle cartridge, the rimfire or the centre-fire. These terms refer to the method in which the cartridge is ignited. When the inexperienced first see a box of .22 ammunition, they are invariably surprised at the tiny size of both bullet and cartridge and find it difficult to believe the warning on the box which states that the ammunition is 'dangerous to a range of one mile'. It should be remembered, however, that the .22 is a highly effective little round and although the round and cartridge are small, they are lethally effective on appropriate game.

The .22, since it is such a small and relatively low powered cartridge, does not generate very high gas pressures and therefore does not require a heavy brass case. The best method for igniting the powder inside the .22 case is to pack the small rim of the thinly drawn brass cartridge case with priming compound. When the firing pin of the rifle strikes the rim, the priming compound explodes, igniting the powder which generates a mass of expanding gases. Being contained within the cartridge case and chamber the gases push the bullet down the barrel as they expand and erupt out of the muzzle of the rifle behind the bullet. It is this explosion of the gases out of the rifle muzzle which produces the crack of rifle fire.

Heavier calibre cartridges have a much greater amount of powder in them and generate a much greater mass of fast expanding gas on firing. It is to contain this high pressure so that the bullet is blasted down the barrel with safety to the handler that the centre-fire cartridge was developed. The cartridge case, which is made of brass, has a heavy base, into which is fitted the cap or primer. When struck by the firing pin of the rifle the cap ignites the powder in the cartridge, which expands with enormous pressure, generating around 3,515 kg per square centimetre.

The base of the cartridge case is also designed with a small groove running around it. This allows the extractor claw of the bolt to grip the case, drawing it out of the chamber for ejection after firing.

The design and construction of a bullet are highly technical operations to achieve the physical properties necessary to deliver the optimum performance on targets as diverse as the soft skin and relative tiny body size of a roebuck, or the hide of an animal as large as a Cape buffalo. The manufacturers of ammunition have spent large sums of money on research in the quest for the best possible design of the bullet in relation to the intended target. An animal which has a soft skin, small bones and a narrow chest cavity would require a bullet to expand and deliver its optimum energy very quickly since the animal's total chest width may be as little as 30 cm in total. On the other hand there are completely different requirements for a bullet designed for deep penetration into heavy-skinned, large-boned, dense-muscled animals where the bullet may have to travel 30 cm before it reaches the vital areas where expansion and energy dissipation are required.

Once the bullet strikes the target and reaches those vital areas, it must, to achieve optimum dissipation of the striking energy, be stopped in its forward motion as quickly as possible. This is achieved by the design of the bullet jacket, the outside shell of the bullet, which is made of hardened metal. The bullet is constructed with a hollow partition inside it filled with lead. There are various configurations of bullets: PPC or Patented Protected Point, Nosler Partition, Dual Core, Alaska and so on. They all have different configurations of jacket wall thickness and lead internal construction. For example, the Nosler Partition has a partition inside separating two different areas of lead core. This results in the front part of the Nosler expanding on impact while the rear core continues its forward momentum, giving a combi-nation of penetration and expansion.

Included in bullet designs are silver tipped, plastic pointed, spiral pointed, round nose, pointed, boat tailed and flat base. All these different design features have their own special perfor-mance characteristics.

Research into the design of bullets has shown that although a pointed bullet, being more streamlined, retains air speed, round-nosed bullets are steadier in flight since they are less easily deflected by striking grass or twigs. All these bullets are referred to as 'soft point' and they are the most commonly used for almost all game shooting. Indeed legislation exists in most countries stipulating the use of soft or hollow pointed bullets for shooting game.

The choice of the right calibre and cartridge for your type of shooting will depend on a number of considerations. First, you must decide on the game species that you will shoot most frequently. If you intend mainly to stalk red deer on the open hill with the occasional roebuck, then you might consider a .270 with a choice of cartridges between 130 gr. and 150 gr. My experience has been that 150 gr. .270 gives excellent performance, felling even the largest stags, whilst causing minimal carcass damage. If, however, you intend to stalk mainly roe deer with an occasional red deer stag, then a .243 would be a better choice, requiring a lighter and smaller bullet at 100 gr. It is superb on roebuck and is certainly perfectly capable of dealing with large stags. In fact my own experience is that, having a preference for my .243, I shoot almost all my stags with it and find it more than adequate for the job.

However, other considerations come into the choice of calibre and cartridge; for example, do you intend to spend any amount of time shooting abroad? Boar, for instance, can be taken with a .243, but my personal choice would be for a .30–06. This would give me a bullet range from 130 gr. up to a massive 200 gr. Again my experience has been that a 180 gr. round stops even the largest boar in his tracks.

What you are looking for in your choice of cartridge is, as I have said, the bullet that is best suited to your own needs, giving you a balance of velocity and performance on target. Although my personal choice would be between the three calibres .243, .270 and .30–06, if I was to choose only one calibre for stalking in Britain, then the choice I would probably make would be .243.

In any discussion on cartridges and calibres, it should always be borne in mind that large calibres, with huge knock-down power, are no substitute for accuracy. As I have previously said, familiarity and practice with your rifle are the only means by which you can confidently place bullets accurately in your quarry. It is every sportsman's absolute responsibility to do everything in his power to kill his quarry as cleanly, humanely and quickly as possible — and that can only be achieved with accuracy.

CHAPTER THREE

Other Equipment

KNIVES

I am often surprised that some sportsmen will spend large sums of money on some of their equipment — their guns, scopes, binoculars, clothing and the various accoutrements of shooting and stalking — yet become positively miserly over the purchase of a knife, often producing, if they have one at all, an inferior, badly maintained, blunt apology for what a knife should be. I do, however, believe that the reason for this is that the average British sportsman neither understands nor fully appreciates what makes a good knife, or indeed has experienced the pleasure of using one.

The British tend to regard a knife as a cheap tool, having little appreciation of the quality end of the market, where the cheap tool is transformed into a finely balanced instrument, beautifully made of the finest materials. The American field sportsman, on the other hand, has long shown a greater appreciation for the knife-maker's art, some knife-makers achieving fame and collectability with the hand-made products of their workshops.

The best possible advice when buying a new knife is, quite simply, buy the most expensive you can afford. But what makes a *good* knife? At its simplest a knife is a cutting edge that will perform for you a particular cutting requirement. However, knives come in various shapes, sizes and forms, ranging from the clumsy and inferior made of poor steel, to instruments of superior design, balance and material, and there is a great deal of difference in what is required to sharpen a pencil, shave your face, skin a rabbit, or gralloch and later skin a large red deer stag.

Knives come in two basic types — sheath or folding. The sheath knife has a permanently fixed blade and must be carried in a leather case or sheath when not in use. It is bigger, heavier and has to be carrried on a belt. The folding knife is carried in your pocket; to use it you fold the blade back until it locks in place (non-lock knives should not be considered). Folding knives are limited to straight blades with a single cutting edge, although there are some more expensive models which feature a Bowie blade. Blade lengths in this chapter are given in Imperial, not metric, measurements, since these are the norm.

The knife consists of four basic parts: blade, tang, handle and sheath. Each of them must conform to various requirements if the knife is to give optimum use to the user.

Blades come in many shapes and sizes. The dagger has a cutting edge on both sides, running to a sharp point. It has little practical purpose and is really only of use as a war weapon. The Royal Marine Commandos use the dagger design, but it is not meant for skinning or butchering their quarry: it is designed purely as a stabbing weapon. With a cutting edge on both sides combined with a needle sharp point it is ideal for driving deep into an opponent's flesh, and because of its tapered shape it can easily be withdrawn with minimal effort before being thrust in again. Having a cutting edge on both sides also means that, once withdrawn from its sheath prior to being used, the user does not have to feel with his other hand to find the cutting edge.

The dagger design is only used in field sports in some European countries, particularly Germany, where quasi-military connections with some of the gamekeepers spilled over into the design of uniforms which, certainly for ceremonial occasions, incorporate a knife of dagger design. They are, however, for practical purposes not worth consideration by the sportsman.

A knife design which has become increasingly popular in recent years is the Japanese tanto. Similar to the Bowie, it has a long blade, sweeping gradually up to a tip, the back of the blade being completely blunt, yet having a slight upward curve toward the tip. The rise in its popularity is the result of an interest in Oriental weapons brought about by the fashion for Kung Fu/ Ninja films which has swept the West. Although a good quality tanto is capable of taking and holding an exceptional edge, for all practical purposes it has no use in the field sportsman's equipment.

The Bowie knife is so called after Jim Bowie, the American frontiersman who died at the Alamo and who is credited with its design. The term 'Bowie' is used to describe all manner of knives which come in an enormous range of lengths and blade weights, all sharing the same characteristic, that of a long blade with a moderate sweep up to the point on the cutting edge. The back of the blade, which is entirely blunt for some two-thirds of its length, then features a cutaway, which can be sharpened.

To be useful, the main edge of the Bowie blade should be of a different cutting configuration from the back. The main edge should be sharpened for general flesh cutting, i.e. to a narrow cutting edge, whereas the back of the blade, used for chopping or rougher work, should have a much wider cutting edge.

The Bowie is not an ideal knife for a field sportsman unless the user is very familiar with it. Being straight, its use is limited to the last quarter of the main blade where it curves up to the point, since that is the part of the blade that is used in skinning. Unless you have use for the straight cutting edge then it is unnecessary and makes the use of the blade more awkward. This is particularly relevant when skinning an animal where you wish to keep the skin, for instance when caping out a stag which you wish to have mounted. To avoid cutting holes which need later stitching, you would do better to use a small curved blade.

The knife blade does not stop where it meets the handle, only the cutting edge does. The steel of the blade continues up into the handle. Some cheap knives have a wedge or spike-shaped tang onto which the handle is glued. This sort of knife should not be considered.

The only knife construction which the sportsman should look for when choosing a knife is one where the blade continues through the centre and is an integral part of the handle, dividing the grips, which should be of a material impervious to temperature change, moisture and reasonable knocking about. The grips, which should be two separate pieces, are best if they have broad brass or metal rivets running through from surface to surface. Handle materials which I recommend are deer antler, resin-impregnated compressed canvas and resin-impregnated compressed wood.

Of great importance when choosing a knife is the presence of a guard between handle and blade. It is important that you have some method of preventing your hand slipping down the blade when wet and cold, with the obvious result. This is the

The author's knives, from the top:

A $7\frac{1}{2}$ in Puma Bowie, heavy and impractical for most purposes. Note the handle has been buffed smaller and smooth for easier use.

A 6 in Puma Bowie, an excellent all-round knife. Note the handle has been buffed smooth for easier use.

A folding Puma with 4 in blade. Excellent all-round knife. Note the handle has been buffed smooth for easier use.

A Westmark with $5\frac{1}{2}$ in blade. This is a big game skinner, excellent in design and use.

A 3 in Condor big game skinner, excellent in design and use.

A $2\frac{1}{2}$ in Condor small game skinner, excellent in design and use.

one principal drawback with all folding knives: they do not incorporate a fixed hand guard.

The fourth consideration is the sheath: there is little point in buying an expensive knife and honing it to a keen edge, then carrying it around in an inferior sheath. Strangely, many manufacturers, having made a knife using finest steel, then fall down on the design of its sheath. Examine the sheath in which you will carry your knife. All too often you will discover that when you remove the blade you are running the cutting edge up the leather of the sheath. Whilst the knife may last you a lifetime, the sheath will not.

Some sheath designs allow the whole handle to protrude. Personally I favour the sheath design where the handle is at least half inside the sheath, or better, a sheath which has a top flap which studs down.

My personal preference is for a Bowie blade, but I have used knives for many years and it would be fair to say have a degree of expertise in their use that the average sportsman would be unlikely to have. When roe stalking I carry one knife, a folding lock knife with a 4 in cutting edge of the Bowie design. When stalking stags I would normally carry my 6 in blade, or alternatively my favourite knife for working on big game – a Westmark, another blade of Bowie design with a 5 in cutting edge which sweeps quite beautifully up to the tip. This blade combines all the characteristics that for me make a superb instrument, being deep across the belly of the blade, the back of the blade being a good 5 mm in thickness. It is strong enough to deal with every conceivable task that one might require of it when working on big game and the steel is of such quality that once sharpened, it holds its edge. It would be fair to say, however, that if you were skinning game smaller than a red deer stag, this blade would prove awkward in the average hand.

So what is the ideal knife for the field sportsman? If he wants to skin animals then he requires a short curved blade. If he wants to chop bone he requires an axe. If he wishes to cut brush when hide building, he requires a machete. If he wishes to sharpen a pencil he requires a penknife and if he wishes to cut his sandwiches he is being over-delicate. In other words, it is not possible in one blade to meet all the tasks which the sportsman might require, for apart from the impracticality of design, a knife sharpened to a razor's edge for skinning and flesh cutting could quickly be damaged if used for rougher work. The sportsman therefore should have a skinning knife which is used for nothing else and in the event of him wanting to cut brush, he should have a separate tool for the job.

Sharpening the knife

There is little point in buying an expensive knife which will come from the manufacturer wonderfully sharp, then through laziness allow the blade to become progressively blunter until it is useless and requires a major honing job. Your new knife will come with an edge, the angle of the V that makes up the actual cutting edge, which is set.

A very narrow V would be for cutting flesh. The wider the sides of the V are, the more the blade is designed for rough work, chopping, etc. It is therefore important when you buy a knife that you also buy a good sharpening stone and that you learn to use it, maintaining the keenness of the edge. Sharpening a knife,

Opposite Buzzards are a common sight to the stalker. They prey on animals up to a medium-sized rabbit, and are also carrion eaters.

however, is not simply a case of rubbing the metal on some rough surface to grind it to an edge. This sort of crude treatment should be avoided.

There are various knife sharpening products available, from the basic carborundum stone to Arkansas stones of varying degrees of fineness. The Arkansas stone is without doubt the finest natural product for the job. However, there are many other sharpening devices available, from diamond dust to glass beads, normally stuck to a handle of some sort. When buying a sharpening stone the same advice applies as when buying your knife: buy the most expensive one you can afford, you will not regret it.

Sharpening a knife is a task which requires a little practice and a degree of skill to reach proficiency. It is not a job which should be attempted hurriedly, but is best carried out in a relaxed fashion when you have the time. If you are using a stone then you must lay it on a table at a comfortable working height and not for instance on a low coffee table. Place it on a pad of newspaper to catch and absorb any drops of the lubricating oil you will have to use on the stone. Examine most carefully the angle at which the cutting edge is set. It is important that you keep this angle. Lightly lay the blade on the stone, holding the handle in your right hand, and with the index finger of your left positioned on the front of the blade, draw the cutting edge across the stone towards yourself. As the cutting edge of the blade nears the tip, you raise the hand which holds the handle slightly, to maintain the same angle of edge. Repeat this manoeuvre three times. Then change hands, taking the knife in your left hand, right index finger on the tip of the blade, and repeat the exercise three times.

The idea is to strop both sides of the blade an equal number of times, gradually reducing the frequency. For example, you may strop the blade in six groups of three, both right and left, reducing to six groups of two, right and left, finishing off with perhaps ten single strops alternating between each side.

The alternative position for sharpening is to sit with the knife held firmly in your hand. Lay the stone gently on the angle of the cutting edge and in tiny circular motions of the stone, slowly work your way down the blade to the tip. Then work down the other side of the blade towards the tip, again in tiny circular motions of the stone, taking care to retain the angle of the edge. I regard my skinning knife as sharp when I can dry shave a small area of my leg or arm with ease. With this standard of keenness of edge, a good knife will slice through flesh with great ease, but should not be used for any other form of rough task, or the keenness of the edge will be lost.

BINOCULARS

A necessary part of every sportsman's equipment is a good pair of binoculars, whether for watching flighting pigeon so that he can establish the line prior to positioning himself, for watching wildfowl at a distance or for examining a stag to ascertain the size and quality of his head prior to a stalk.

The inexperienced naturally assume that the more powerful the magnification of a pair of binoculars, the more use it will be to him. Indeed the opposite is the case. Binoculars, if they are to be of real use to the sportsman, should have a combination of good magnification so that he can examine a distant object and good light gathering properties so that they may be used in bad light conditions (early morning or at gathering dusk), and be light-weight enough that they can be carried with ease. If the magnification is too great the user will quickly get eye strain and a headache. In addition, the greater the magnification the greater the effect will be of the user's natural shaking or vibration. Therefore binoculars of anything more than $8 \times$ should not be considered. The wise sportsman would restrict himself to glasses of either $7 \times$ or $8 \times$. My own glasses are 7×42 Leitz and I find them superb in every way. The only drawback is that they are expensive.

A good illustration of the above occurred when I was stalking with a fellow who was carrying a large, fancy-looking pair of binoculars of $12 \times$. We lay down to watch some distant stags. I remarked that the stag on the left had nice cups on top of his antlers. My companion couldn't make them out. Eventually we exchanged glasses, and whilst his were certainly powerful, it was virtually impossible to hold them still enough to examine the distant object. Mine, on the other hand, with lower power were infinitely superior and a joy to use.

CHAPTER FOUR

Small Game

The grey squirrel (*Sciurus carolinensis*)

The smallest species found in Britain that the sportsman might shoot and eat is the grey squirrel. Regarded in the United States as the best eating of all small game, the grey squirrel tends to be disregarded in Britain and treated purely as vermin. If shot it is shot as a pest and discarded. They grey squirrel has become part of the British countryside, having spread almost throughout the whole of the British Isles since its introduction from the United States and subsequent escape from various locations during the latter quarter of the nineteenth century and the first quarter of the twentieth.

The grey squirrel has spread and multiplied rapidly and is now to be found in most parts of England and Wales, Ireland and as far north as the central highlands of Scotland. In some areas, particularly in the south of England, they have become so dense that they are regarded as an infestation. One of the reasons the grey squirrel has multiplied virtually unchecked is the absence of natural predators, unlike in the United States where several species of birds of prey hunt them. The only creature in Britain capable of catching and eating the grey squirrel is the pine marten and they are now so rare other than in the north of Scotland that the two species seldom meet.

The grey squirrel should not be confused with the red squirrel which is protected. The grey is a rodent of medium size which has a long bushy tail, almost half the total length of the animal. It has dense grey fur with an overbloom of reddish yellow on back and flanks, with white underparts. The grey squirrel can change coat colour from a shorter summer coat which normally

has a brownish tinge to a grey or silver-grey dense winter coat. Unlike his red British cousin the grey does not have ear tufts.

Goshawks are the supreme woodland avian predators of small game. Though rare in Britain, their numbers are increasing.

If you have grey squirrels on your land you would be advised to eradicate them. They are a vermin species and can do considerable damage to birds' eggs and be destructive to some species of trees.

The best shot size for grey squirrel is 7, or if using a rifle the recommended calibre is .22.

Rabbit (*Oryctolagus cuniculus*)

Throughout the countryside of England one occasionally comes across the name 'warren' as in names like Upper Warren or Warren-on-Hill, and in medieval literature one comes across names like Sir John of the Warren. All these names originate from the warrens where rabbit populations were established, most likely by the Normans as a food source — if you like, the forerunner of intensive farming. Walled enclosures were established to keep the rabbits captive. They were of course easily husbanded and harvested whenever their meat was required for the table. This situation would appear to have remained stable for some time, since reports of rabbits in the wild do not feature until around the mid-1800s.

The rabbit is not indigenous to Britain but originated from North Africa and southern Europe. When rabbits started to find their way out of captivity the population multiplied at great speed, until the rabbit was to be found throughout Britain. The rabbit is a food source species, by which I mean it is an animal which multiplies at great speed to accommodate its predators. Of course in Britain there were not sufficient predators to deal with the rabbit's considerable reproductive powers. Therefore the population continued to expand until it reached the point where large areas of Britain were almost overrun. Whilst this ever-growing bountiful and delicious meat source was appreciated by the general population of Britain, both human and predatory bird and animal, it caused enormous damage to agriculture. During the first half of the twentieth century the rabbit may have provided a welcome source of food, particularly during the two World Wars, but it was, however, also putting intolerable and vastly expensive pressure on farmers.

The development of the disease myxomatosis was greatly welcomed by agricultural interests, and when it was first introduced in the mid-1950s this form of germ-warfare swept through the rabbit population with astonishing speed and virulence, the population being almost wiped out by the epidemic. Such was the initial relief of the farming community that the horror of the suffering from this hellish disease was not at first considered. Only after rabbits had been seen sitting about starving, their heads massively swollen, the pus-filled ulcerations around their eyes rendering them blind, was the full enormity of what the disease represented realized by the majority of caring countrymen. I very much doubt that, if such a disease were developed today, public opinion would allow its use.

The rabbit population, however, was not completely eradicated. Small groups of survivors of the disease were left, so the rabbit numbers started to build again. This is the case at the present day in areas which have a rabbit population. They multiply dramatically in the spring when the weather and sources of food are coming to their best and can support a growing population. But before they become other than a localized problem, myxomatosis, which has been dormant since the previous year, reappears, reducing their numbers. This normally coincides with an increase in colder, damp weather around autumn, when the rabbits are more likely to be numerous and huddled in burrows, conditions in which the disease can be spread quickly.

Agriculture and field sports normally manage to coexist and indeed are often complementary to each other, but in the case of rabbits, the farming community has no interest in seeing them on their ground. The average farmer, if given his choice, would have no rabbits whatever. The field sportsman who shoots on an area which has a rabbit population must understand the position he is in. If he were to shoot rabbits as sparingly as he would any other game species, then he would be inviting the farmer to take further steps to protect his interests, either by insisting on a greater cull or worst of all by taking matters into his own hands and gassing the population.

I therefore recommend fairly hard shooting on rabbits. It is extremely unlikely that they could be eradicated by shooting alone but the number taken is something which the individual must decide in relation to his own special circumstances. If the rabbits on my own ground are becoming noticeably numerous — which they tend to do in one particular area — then I occasionally enlist the assistance of a friend who has ferrets and we either bolt the rabbits from their burrows using the ferrets, which can be exciting sport; alternatively, we ferret them into nets. In this way the farmer sees that we are doing something about the numbers.

The rabbit eats a wide variety of grasses, plants and shoots, and can do extensive damage to arable crops and domestic gardens. Rabbits, in common with many herbivores, practise a habit known as refection. This means that they eat some of their droppings in order to extract any nutrients not digested first time around. By sniffing their droppings they can tell whether they are completely digested or contain nutrients.

A feature of an area which contains rabbits is their latrine. It is easily spotted, and normally located on a mound or even on top of a rock, where you will see a liberal scattering of droppings. Any grass growing there will be badly yellowed and burnt by the acidity in the urine.

The shot size I recommend for rabbits is 5 or 6, with a .22 rifle, or, if using a rifle, the recommended calibre is .22.

Brown hare (*Lepus capensis europaeus*)

Sportsmen's attitudes to hares vary considerably. Many sportsmen like hares and do not wish to shoot them, whilst others will shoot them without real appreciation of the animal. This is largely due, I believe, to the lack of culinary appreciation of the hare in the British shooting household, for whilst the rabbit, being pale of flesh and relatively mild in flavour, is easily cooked even by the inexperienced, the hare, being a red meat of stronger flavour, requires a little more care and knowledge if the potential of this delicious game animal is to be fully exploited. Sadly a high percentage of hares shot are either sold or fed to dogs. The shooter, if questioned, would often say that he only shoots an occasional hare as a treat for his dogs since he does not like eating them. The real reason is not so much that he does not like eating them, but that he does not know how to cook them.

The hare is an attractive looking animal, with a rich russet brown coat on his shoulders, neck and flanks which often have black tips on the guard hairs or an over-colouring of brown or grey, with a white belly. Particularly noticeable with the hare are the very long ears which are black tipped, as is the upper part of the tail. With large pronounced eyes, the hare could truly be described as a handsome animal. The eyes are positioned well out on either side of the head to give an enormously wide field of vision. They can also act independently of each other, allowing a hare to see in two directions at the same time. Although hares have an average weight of 4 kg, people are normally surprised when they see their first shot hare since it appears so large, the reason being that it has a long, narrow body.

The hare's preferred environment is open country and light woodland, where it can find a ready supply of the wide range of shoots and grasses which it eats, and the cover that it prefers. Territorial animals, a hare will normally stay within a given range of some four to ten fields. Although it is capable of travelling several miles and will freely enter water and swim across rivers to an attractive food source, if undisturbed the hare would usually inhabit a localized area.

The term 'mad as a March hare' is a good description of the behaviour of buck hares during the springtime breeding season. These normally solitary, retiring animals then congregate in numbers – anything from two or three up to as many as ten or twelve – and will often behave in the most bizarre fashion, leaping and kicking, boxing and generally jumping over each other in apparent oblivion to everything else. They can often be approached and observed quite closely whilst indulging in this annual ritual.

The young of hares are known as leverets and are normally born through spring and summer in litters of four. Hares can breed throughout the year, though they are most active during the warmer months when food is more freely available. If the latter part of summer has been good, a late litter of hares may be seen when shooting in the early part of the season. Hares were at one time more numerous than they are now. However, changing farming practices and the use of pesticides have had an adverse effect on the hare population.

As I have emphasized previously, it is imperative that the good game shot understands the limitations of his range and is willing to exercise restraint from shooting at anything which may be at a questionable distance. Indeed, if he is in any doubt at all he must give the animal the benefit of the doubt and hold his fire. It is unfortunate that when shooting hares some people are misled by the hare's large size into thinking that it is closer than it is. Add to this the shooter's unwillingness to accept the limitation of his

Running leveret.

Brown hare.

shotgun range and the result is the unnecessary shooting and wounding of hares who are just too far away.

The shot size for brown hare is 4 or 5; if using a rifle the recommended calibre is .22.

The Scottish or blue hare
(*Lepus timidus scoticus*)

The 'blue' in the name of this hare refers to the colour of its summer coat; it is also known as the white hare, a reference to its winter coat. Living in the high heather-clad mountain areas of Scotland, the animal takes on as camouflage the colour of the heather in spring and summer, gradually changing in the autumn to blend in with the winter snows. It is not a true blue but rather a brownish blue and is excellent camouflage, as is the white coat when on a snow background. White hares often allow you to approach them very closely, since being camouflaged, by sitting motionless, danger often passes them by. Their white coats are wonderful protection against the cold weather since the fur traps tiny air bubbles as insulation.

Similar to its larger lowland cousin, the brown hare, the blue hare is a solitary animal. In the areas of Wales, northern England and Ireland where they have been introduced, they are doing well.

For many years the white hare was ignored as a sporting species because of the inaccessibility of its habitat. Visiting guns were only likely ever to see it when they were shooting grouse or stalking. The idea of shooting blue hare, other than the occasional one either for the table or the dog, was never discussed. Consequently, the animal bred in vast numbers. The only natural predators it had were eagles, foxes and wildcats, and since the keepers controlled the numbers of foxes and wildcats legally and the eagles illegally, the hare population reached enormous proportions.

As a result the practice of hare drives became the norm on most highland estates up until the mid-1970s. These hare drives comprised guns, numbering anything from ten to twenty, joining in what was essentially a population cull. Standing guns had the hares driven towards them by walking guns who took in large areas of the hill, driving the hares in front of them. Huge bags numbering many hundreds were shot in the day. This annual cull, although distasteful to present-day field sportsmen, was necessary and continued for many years.

The end of hare drives coincided with the increase in sporting lets on the highland estates. Up until the 1970s estates were shot over either by the owners, their guests or individuals who leased the estate for the season. However, with the upsurge in the number of shooting lets being taken by the week and the greater numbers of sportsmen demanding shooting, particularly sportsmen from all over Europe, attention was drawn to this apparently endless supply of sporting animals for which the Europeans were willing to pay substantial sums to shoot. Overnight the drives became a thing of the past.

With an unseemly attitude of greed and lack of consideration for wildlife, the highland estates grabbed this new source of income, doing little or nothing to protect the continuity of the game supply, and the hares were shot very hard, with no thought to their reproduction. Add to this a series of severe winters in the highlands in the late 1970s and early 1980s and the population was decimated, and has never fully recovered. Indeed, I believe it never will, until the shooting of this species ceases, at least for a few years.

The shot size for the blue hare is 4 or 5; if using a rifle the recommended calibre is .22.

The Irish hare (*Lepus timidus hibernicus*)

The Irish hare is common in the mountain areas of Ireland and is a most attractive animal, with its russet coloured coat. The Irish hare does turn white in winter but the coat change and disguise is not as efficient as the Scottish hare, the white being less uniform. Larger than the blue hare, they are solitary animals, although they have the peculiarity of congregating during the breeding season in large numbers, sometimes in excess of 200.

The shot size for the Irish hare is 4 or 5; if using a rifle the recommended calibre is .22.

Buzzard.

CHAPTER FIVE

Large Game

DEER

There are six species of deer found in Britain: muntjac, Chinese water deer, roe deer, fallow deer, sika deer and, the largest, red deer.

The muntjac and Chinese water deer are recent additions to the stalker's game list. These small oriental deer have grown in number and range and are now found in many areas.

Of all the big game in the world, there is no animal that has provided as much sport and food than the deer in its many species. Since the earliest times that men have hunted game, first simply to eat, then eventually for both food and sport, the deer has represented the very essence of hunting. The deer is in legend, art and literature. Jealously guarded for the privileged few, the taking of a deer was a capital offence during medieval times. Today in Britain the deer is protected by a series of laws and statutes against taking it with inappropriate weapons, outside the specified season, or without permission.

Deer have managed to adapt to the changing countryside and our constant invasion of the wilderness areas. Although the public's image of deer in Britain is of herds roaming the high mountains of Scotland far from human habitation, deer are also found in the most unlikely places. Within the city boundary of Glasgow, if you know where to look, you will find roe deer. Within 40 kilometres of the city centre fallow deer can be found, as can red deer. Roe and fallow deer also live within a few kilometres of London.

What is it that so attracts men to stalk deer today? They are highly attuned to survival in their environment with superb hearing and sense of smell, and to stalk one successfully is an achievement. I have never met a true stalker who did not have a great affection for the deer and it would be true to say that the best stalkers are the most enthusiastic students of their habits and habitat. If carefully managed and shot responsibly deer are a regenerative animal and constantly provide a source of sport.

One important aspect of stalking deer is the wonderful venison they provide. There is no other meat which is quite so delicious on the table — and no meat tastes as well as that which you have provided yourself.

Male deer of course have antlers, an attractive memento to commemorate a successful stalk. Since earliest times, antlers have been collected as trophies of the chase to decorate walls and make the statement that the owner is a successful stalker.

The Chinese or Reeve's muntjac
(*Muntiacus reevesi*)
and the
Indian muntjac (*Muntiacus muntjac*)

The male is known as a buck, the female as a doe and the young as a fawn.

There are two species of muntjac found in the United Kingdom, though in their southern Asian home the muntjac comprises five species and fifteen sub-species. It was originally brought to this country during the late nineteenth century as a curiosity for private collections. Inevitably animals escaped into the surrounding countryside, where they formed the basis of what was to become the wild population.

The muntjac is sometimes known as the barking deer, a reference to their single bark which they may give at about five second intervals, sometimes for thirty minutes or more. This barking is normally emitted when the deer is alarmed. Muntjac are higher in their hind quarters than at the shoulder. The bucks grow antlers protruding from long skin-covered pedicles, to a length of 6 to 7.5 cm. The bucks have small pronounced sharp tusks. They have a rich reddish chestnut body with a darker back. If alarmed, as they depart, both bucks and does will raise their tails, which are about 15 cm long, which display the white undersides.

They are small animals, the Indian buck being an average

Muntjac are so small and secretive that they often go unnoticed.

57 cm at the shoulder and weighing about 13 kg. The doe stands at 50 cm at the shoulder and weighs about $11-11\frac{1}{2}$ kg. The Reeve's buck averages 45 cm at the shoulder, weighing about 11 kg. The doe is about 38 cm at the shoulder and weighs about 10 kg.

Muntjac are highly secretive, living singly or in pairs. They are now spread from the south of England in pockets to north of Sheffield, and can be found in areas around the English/Welsh border as well as some east coast areas, Norfolk for example.

The muntjac is highly adept at living unnoticed by man. As an example of this, whilst I was visiting a rural area outside of Stratford-upon-Avon, it struck me that the garden of my host and the surrounding countryside looked like it might hold a few muntjac, and after an early morning investigation we spotted several. My host, being unaware of the wildlife, had lived in that house for many years without ever having seen the little deer. Only after I revealed that if he wanted to see them he should get up early in the morning, and gave him instructions on how to approach the ground, did he see them for the first time.

The muntjac has a distinctive musky odour which is not unpleasant and can normally be identified on territorial rubbing points. Their droppings are usually found in latrine areas and are less than 1 cm long in the shape of small black pellets.

If you are looking for muntjac tracks you should try areas

of soft mud. They are about 3 cm long, narrow and pointed. In areas which they use regularly muntjac form runs or access tracks which, since they are invariably through long vegetation, give the appearance of tunnels.

The muntjac, in common with the roe, forms family groups of buck and doe together with that year's fawn. The fawn remains with them until the doe is ready to drop her next fawn; she then drives the yearling away.

There are now a few areas in Britain where the muntjac population has become so numerous as to afford some selective culling, although personally I find the presence of these little deer an attractive addition to the environment and would only recommend shooting them if the local population can sustain the loss. In areas where they are rare, it would be inadvisable to take any, unless the intention is to discourage their spread.

The recommended rifle calibre for shooting muntjac is .243.

Although I have watched muntjac on many occasions I have never shot one.

The Chinese water deer (*Hydropotes inermis*)

The male is known as a buck, the female as a doe and the young as a fawn.

The Chinese water deer is similar in appearance to the muntjac, being higher behind, but without antlers. The bucks have prominent tusks, about 5–6 cm long. They are similar in colour to the muntjac being reddish brown in summer, whilst in winter they grow a coat with a greyer overall look. The tail is about half the length (7.5 cm) of the muntjac's. They normally keep it tucked tight in and in running off no white is shown.

The buck stands about 49–52 cm at the shoulder and weighs an average of 12 kg. The doe is slightly smaller, being 48–50 cm at the shoulder and weighs an average of 10 kg.

It is difficult to distinguish between the droppings and the tracks of muntjac and water deer. Both sexes have a distinctive bark which they use principally as a signal of alarm.

The Chinese water deer, like the muntjac and roe, forms family groups of buck and doe together with that year's fawn which remains with them until the doe is ready to drop her next fawn. She drives the yearling away.

In Britain Chinese water deer are mainly to be found in East Anglia, Hampshire, Buckinghamshire, Shropshire and Bedfordshire. Although there are reports of them being seen outside these areas, such reports are difficult to substantiate since other than to the expert eye they can be mistaken for the more common muntjac.

As with the muntjac, I feel that these little deer should only be shot if numbers allow, or if for some reason you wish to reduce the population.

The recommended calibre for Chinese water deer is .243.

Although I have watched Chinese water deer I have never shot one.

Roe deer (*Capreolus capreolus*)

The male is known as a buck, the female as a doe and the young as a kid, although the latter is often incorrectly referred to as a fawn.

The roe deer is the most beautiful and the smallest of our indigenous British deer. So attractive and widespread is this delightful animal that many books and studies have been devoted to it. The roe is found in almost every country throughout Europe, and there are different species across Siberia and through China.

As a species the roe in Britain has evolved little since prehistoric times. Whilst the tunnels for the new Victoria Line under London were being dug the fossilized remains of a roe were found, showing the animal to be virtually unchanged to the present day.

Roe have also roamed Scotland since prehistoric times, though different periods have seen the population in areas reduced, largely due to excessive hunting for its succulent meat. During the eighteenth and nineteenth centuries the roe was virtually wiped out in most of the Scottish lowland counties. Augmented by the introduction of roe in Ayrshire at the Culzean Estate, the surviving population has regenerated itself and today there is not a county in the whole of Scotland where roe cannot be found, from the mountain areas of the highlands to the rich wooded valleys of the lowlands.

Unfortunately the roe population of England did not fare so well as in Scotland and was believed by many authorities during the eighteenth and nineteenth centuries to be extinct. This is unlikely to have been the case since the England of those times was heavily wooded and relatively lightly populated. The likelihood of the roe having been completely eradicated from the north of England, particularly around the Lake District and Furness Fells, is highly improbable. It was, however, almost certain to have been extinct in the south of England.

Petworth Estate in Sussex is credited as being the locale of the successful reintroduction of roe into England around 1800, though Milton Abbas in Dorset introduced roe around the same time. Enthusiastic estate owners aided the natural spread of the animal by introducing specimens to their own areas, notably Thetford in Norfolk around the mid-1880s. Such is the ability of the roe to colonize any suitable area if given a chance that the population has spread with great success throughout the whole of southern England.

The roe is not found in Wales. Although at one time native to Wales no roe have been reported there for over 300 years. They were never indigenous to Ireland; during the latter part of the nineteenth century a number of roe from Perthshire were introduced to Ireland and were highly successful on a localized basis. Some of the bucks from County Sligo produced phenomenal antler growth with one head having twelve points, and the roe population flourished there for a number of years before they were shot out in the early part of the twentieth century.

Probably as a result of their small size and the absence of the type of spectacular antler growth that one sees in larger species of deer, the roe was not regarded as challenging sporting quarry in Britain until recent years. In medieval times the roe was likened to the hare and was referred to as a 'beast of the warren', to be hunted by the clergy and lower social ranks. Indeed up until the mid-1960s anyone displaying an interest in stalking roe was regarded as a bit of an oddball. The common practice was to have roe drives, the beasts being shot with shotguns. This was intended partly as a population controlling exercise, with the animals providing a source of meat.

Around 1960 the numbers of Continental stalkers coming to Britain to shoot started to increase. These early European visitors must have thought they had discovered the land of milk and honey for whilst the roe was highly regarded in Europe and stalking not easy to come by, here in Britain these visitors could shoot as many roe as they wished, often for no more payment than a bottle of whisky or a few pounds to the farmer or

Roebuck and doe.

landowner. At the same time British stalkers were becoming more aware of roe as stalking became more popular in Britain, particularly with a wider social grouping. Therefore demand for stalking and appreciation of roe quickly increased. Never slow to see a source of income, British sporting estates quickly changed their attitude to roe, modelling their costs and trophy assessment on the European system.

The roe has two distinct coat changes per year. In summer the coat is a bright foxy red with a light texture, with a paler, sand coloured belly. In October the coat becomes much thicker, developing a dark brown-grey colouring, still with the sandy colour belly. Two bands of greyish white often develop on the throat in the winter coat. In winter the caudal disk beneath the rump becomes a distinctive white which, when the roe is alarmed and running, is flared as a danger signal.

Both the mature buck and doe are approximately the same size, about 63–75 cm at the shoulder, weighing between 20 and 30 kg. In common with all deer, weight and condition is dependent on the available food and the environment in which they live. Open hillside tends to provide less in the way of immediately available nutrients, and the more exposed environment requires the animal to utilize more of its natural fats to maintain body temperature. Conversely, a sheltered woodland surrounding would be less exposed, requiring less use of body fats, and at the same time the amount of food available would be greater.

The roe track is distinctive and once you are familiar with it you quickly learn to read details such as whether the deer was walking, trotting or running. When walking, the slot is about 3–4 cm wide at the heel running forward to a neat point, both cleaves (toes) being together, and 4–5 cm in length. The stride is from 66–69 cm. When trotting the cleaves open. When running the cleaves are splayed and the dew claw tracks can be clearly seen. The stride varies, depending on the urgency of the flight and the animal's size and fitness, but would be in groups of four, about 2 metres or more apart.

Droppings when fresh are a shiny dark brown/black, about $1\frac{1}{2}$–2 cm in length and oval.

During winter the buck is antlerless, having dropped them during November/December, and until the growth of the new antlers is clearly visible, the sexes can easily be mistaken. One feature during this period that distinguishes the sexes is the doe's anal tush, a long tuft of hair clearly visible and often incorrectly described as a tail. By spring the buck has cleaned off the velvet of his antlers.

Both bucks and does have a loud bark which is normally only emitted when disturbed. Kids have a 'peep'. During the rut the doe will give a piping call.

Although forming a family group bucks and does are not seen together throughout the year. Being more secretive than the doe, the buck will remain in the vicinity of the doe and kids, although

up to a kilometre away, and the normal sight of roe is of the doe with her two offspring. The doe normally has twins (triplets are not unusual) and they will remain with her until she is ready to drop the following year's young. At that time she will chase the yearlings away.

Bucks are highly territorial and come the rut will chase away any young bucks, including their own offspring, in the defence of their territories. The rut is between July and August and has quite a bit of ceremony. The doe often runs in rings or figures of eight, and the buck follows her, with his nose under her tail and making audible sniffing sounds. The rings made as they run are often called 'fairy rings'.

Although not herd animals groups of roe up to six in number may be seen grazing together during the winter months.

If you have roe on your ground, then it is wise before you shoot any to do a good study of the deer on the ground. Assess the number and quality of the deer before deciding which beasts should be shot and when. Some areas will have a resident population with less likelihood of infill from surrounding areas,

Early morning is the best time to see roe in a meadow by the woodland's edge.

which may be too distant, whilst other areas often have a constant infill of young beasts looking for new territories and much depends on the situation on your ground. If you are not knowledgeable enough to assess your roe potential, then the best advice would be to seek assistance from someone who has the knowledge and experience to give advice. If you do not know such a person, then I would advise that you contact the local branch of the Deer Society.

The recommended calibre for shooting roe is .243.

Of the many roe I have stalked, one comes to mind as having been particularly difficult since he was lying pretty well in the open and needed only to stand up to see me.

During the filming of the programme *Roebuck Stalking* I had stalked many roe, on each occasion accompanied by a cameraman equipped with a large camera. For sound I wore a small button mike, so sensitive that it could pick up even my most gentle whisper, transmitting it to the sound engineer with his box of tricks half a kilometre behind me. We had been desperately searching over a period of almost a year for what we could regard as a really excellent buck who would oblige us by being out in the open so that we could stalk him with maximum effect for the camera.

In Sussex, at Petworth Estate, one morning I spotted a superb buck at the edge of an oak wood, at the far end of a field of young grain. He was lying in a patch of thistles and looked as if he fitted the bill perfectly for age, size and location. I started down the field with the cameraman at my shoulder. Every step had to be made with the greatest of care as we slowly neared the beast. Through my scope when I stopped for a quick look I could see him wiggling his ears at the flies. If I could see him all he had to do was turn his head and he could see me.

For filming it was necessary that I get as close as possible, and I always liked to be within 45 metres. When I was 60 metres away and walking with the utmost care, I suddenly noticed a movement in the grass between myself and the buck. It was a fox and it stopped to look at me as the cameraman frantically and silently tried to focus and film. The fox slipped away and we had no sooner resumed our stalk and reduced the distance to 50 metres than to my great alarm a doe walked out beside the buck, turned and looked straight at me. I froze, knowing the cameraman behind would have done the same. Yet I couldn't resist the quietest whisper into my mike that I must have made the strangest looking tree she had ever seen as I stood frozen. Then she turned and stepped daintily away.

I moved closer. Still the buck lay down. I knew if he saw me, in one bound he would be in the undergrowth. I was acutely aware of even the tiniest sound. My breathing seemed incredibly loud. I was less than 40 metres away and could see only his antlers and ears. Then suddenly he stood up and stepped forward. He was walking after the doe. I waited a few seconds, praying the camera was focused. I was tracking the buck in my scope. I made a kissing sound. He stopped for an instant and I squeezed the trigger.

The sequence turned out to be one of the most unique sequences of stalking ever filmed, largely due to the abilities of the cameraman, partly due to my marksmanship, but mostly due to the buck, who unwittingly immortalized himself.

Fallow deer (*Dama dama*)

The male is known as a buck, the female as a doe and the young as a fawn.

The fallow has its origins in the Mediterranean area and although records do not exist for verification, it is probable that the fallow was first brought to Britain by the Romans as a food course.

Such practice in the Old World was common. When they sailed around the Americas the conquistadors were known to have charted islands with fresh water and a supply of fruit. They also introduced pigs to the islands, to multiply as a ready food supply for any passing ships from their own country. These were the ancestors of the wild pig on some of the islands off America.

One must remember that much of the Britain of Roman times was covered in trees, the ideal habitat for deer, and the fallow quickly established itself and multiplied so that by the twelfth century the fallow was very much part of the natural fauna. Today fallow are common in most counties of England, but undoubtedly the finest population of fallow is in the areas surrounding Petworth Estate in Sussex. The estate has 280 hectares of walled-in deer park, in which lives the finest herd of fallow in Britain, some might say in the western hemisphere. Outside the walled park, the rich woodland areas, patchworked with lush arable land, are ideal conditions for the wild fallow to flourish.

The quality of the wild fallow in this area has been augmented by occasional escapees from the park.

Fallow are occasionally found in Wales, and although they are not found throughout Scotland there are areas where they are numerous. Their continued success is due partly to the environment and also partly to the management of their numbers in the areas where they are found.

Unlike the red deer the fallow does not favour an open hill environment. The weather is too harsh and the lack of cover is unattractive to the fallow, which prefers dense woodland. They do not do well in coniferous woodland and whenever they have been introduced into such areas they tend not to stay, their preference being mixed conifer and deciduous or plain deciduous woodland. Fallow are often found on the fringes of woodland, where they break out onto the open hill, particularly if areas of bracken are available to afford the animal the camouflage it needs to avoid detection. Unlike the red deer which gallops away if disturbed, the fallow flees in a series of bounces with all four feet leaving the ground together — probably part of an alarm mechanism. This peculiar action of the fallow as it bounds away is known as 'pronking'. The fallow does, however, also have the normal series of gaits of the deer, i.e. walk, trot, canter and gallop.

Fallow tracks are about 5 cm wide at the heel and of a balanced medium length. The walking stride is about 53 cm. The stride when galloping depends on the animal's size, speed and the terrain over which it is travelling, but on average a galloping fallow will leave tracks in groups of four, about 110 cm between each group. The dew claws are rarely seen in tracks.

The droppings, 1.5 cm long, are black and shiny when fresh and may be found along the track, having been deposited as the animal moves. They can sometimes be found in piles although the animal does not make a latrine. The droppings may be faceted and are pointed at one end and flat (does) or concave (bucks) at the other.

There are three basic colour groups of fallow: the black (or melanistic), the white and the typical fallow. In summer the typical fallow has a fawn coat with white spots; in winter it grows a greyish brown coat, normally grading from dark brown/black on its back to a grey belly. In winter there is little spotting to be seen on these coats. The white is sometimes incorrectly referred to as an albino — the only time an animal can be called an albino is when it is not only completely white, but also has pink eyes.

Opposite The author with a fallow buck.

Fallow buck, part of the
Petworth herd.

In the wild the darker strain is dominant. Examples of white and fawn are seen although they are less common. However, the concentration of several colour strains of animals in park situations gives a wider variety of colours, ranging from a creamy colour through various tones of sand or gold, to a grey, often with silvery tinges, and to a dark brownish black.

The group of fallow known as menil, are particularly pretty. They are a lighter fawn colour than the typical fallow with prominent spots. In their winter coat they become greyish brown, with less visible, though still discernible, spotting.

During the rut fallow bucks have a most distinctive groan rather than a roar. This groan is often repeated at short intervals, sometimes giving the impression of a clicking noise. The doe can bark when alarmed but for calling her fawn has a soft bleat. The fawn in return makes a high-pitched bleat.

Two noticeable features of the fallow buck are his highly prominent Adam's apple and his tail, up to 16 cm long. The fallow is the only deer in Britain to grow palmated antlers. (Palmated means that the antlers of mature bucks grow flattened like the palm of your hand.) The first antlers grown by the fallow are small spikes and yearlings are known as prickets. The second growth of antlers may be palmated, but equally may be round branches. The antler palmation normally appears, if not in the second, then during the third growth, and as the buck ages the antlers grow progressively larger wider palms. Fallow bucks are in their prime when the animal is 9 or 10 years old. The antlers are normally clean of velvet by September and are shed during April/May.

There is little size variation between the sexes. A fully grown mature buck will stand anything from 82–96 cm at the shoulder, with does being 81–87 cm at the shoulder. The average weight of a buck is between 55–64 kg; does are 43–52 kg. In common

The largest fallow buck the author has shot. Note the top tines have been worn off.

with all deer, weight and condition is dependent on feeding and the environment in which they live. A more exposed environment requires the animal to utilize more of its natural fats to maintain body temperature. Conversely, a sheltered woodland surrounding would be less exposed, requiring less use of body fats, and at the same time the food would be more abundant.

Fallow are highly gregarious. Adult bucks congregate in herds for part of the year, living separately from the does, yearlings and fawns, who also form herds. The two groups gravitate towards each other at the rut which takes place around mid-October. Depending on weather conditions, feed and condition of herd, the rut may start at the end of September or can be delayed until early November.

Fallow stalking is available on some estates in Scotland although the quality of the heads is poor and does not compare with the trophy bucks found in England. This is partly due to the quality of the stock, but is also a result of poorer feeding and shelter.

The recommended calibre for shooting fallow is .243 or .270.

I was stalking fallow as a guest on a friend's estate some years ago. Having stalked in to three highly shootable beasts, there was little to choose between them, as they were all approximately of the same age, condition and antler size. Eventually,

A superb fallow buck with does.

after having lain studying the three bucks for some time, I detected what I saw to be a stiffness in the hind quarters of one buck which I assumed probably had an old injury or perhaps rheumatic problems. He therefore made the selection for me and I shot him.

He had a particularly attractive skin, so I carefully skinned him and sent the skin to be dressed. In due course I got the skin back and kept it at home. I was later visited by an acquaintance, a well-known academic and expert in Japanese armour, who was most impressed when he saw the skin. He was so taken with it that I gave it to him as a gift. Imagine my surprise some time later when I found out that the expert was using the skin as a cover for a priceless Japanese armour chest which he claimed had a long illustrious history!

Sika deer (*Cervus nippon*)

The male is known as a stag, the female as a hind and the young as a calf.

The sika, as its Latin name, *Cervus nippon*, tells us, is a red deer from Japan. Sika are found throughout eastern Asia, and were brought to Britain in the late 1800s as an addition to our deer parks, stately homes and private collections.

Inevitably some managed to escape and today we have healthy populations of sika in the south of England, Surrey, Sussex, Somerset, Kent, Hampshire, Devon, Dorset and Wiltshire. They are also found in Oxford, Lancashire and Yorkshire. In Scotland there are distinct areas where the sika are found: Caithness and Sutherland, around Inverness-shire, on the east coast in Angus and Fife, on the west in Argyllshire, and the border area, notably around Selkirk and Peeblesshire. The sika is now very much a part of British fauna and in areas which it has colonized, particularly if there are large areas of their preferred habitat of woodland, it is quite numerous.

Sika are secretive animals and are largely nocturnal. Only in areas where disturbance is minimal will they start to move around so they can be freely seen during the day.

The sika is a brownish red with indistinct buffish yellow spotting on its flanks in its summer coat. In winter its coat is denser, with dark brown on the back, grading down to a brown with grey tinges on the belly. The sika has a prominent white caudal patch, bordered in black. When alarmed or running the sika flares the patch which is quite noticeable.

I always get the impression that sika tracks are slightly larger than one would expect. Rounded at the toe or tip of the hoof, they broaden back to the heel. Big stags' tracks reach up to 7–8 cm in length by 5 cm in width. To add to the confusion, their feet seem more likely to spread in soft ground, giving the impression that the hoof is bigger than it actually is.

Their droppings are black, currant-like and small, although when fresh, they may have a greenish colour. Sika droppings may be found anywhere where the animals have been, although they do tend to use regular soiling points.

The antlers are clean of velvet by September and dropped during April/May. Mature stags have much smaller antlers than their larger red cousins. A mature stag would not normally grow more than eight points, although exceptional beasts may have ten.

Stags range in size from 80–86 cm at the shoulder and weigh 50–64 kg. Hinds are slightly smaller, 75–81 cm at the shoulder, and weigh 38–45 kg.

Rutting normally takes place during October, although it may extend from late September to November. In common with red deer the rut seems to be delayed until the onset of the first frosts. The stags have a distinctive whistling call, although during the rut their voice deepens and sounds more roar-like. The hind has a quiet bleat, while the calf makes a sound which would be best described as a 'peep'.

The sika is less herd-orientated than the red or fallow. The stags, outside of the rut, form into small herds of anything up to twenty in number. The hinds and calves form smaller herds of anything from three or four animals to fifteen.

There are several areas where sika stalking is available.

The rifle calibre for shooting sika is .243 or .270.

Some years ago I was stalking sika on an area overlooking Loch Ness. It was one of these grey days when visibility fluctuated from being good to dropping to less than 100 metres. The mists, as they came by, could fairly be described as being like curtains being drawn across the countryside.

I had been invited to go stalking by a young English merchant banker who had recently decided to escape the rigours of the city and, using his obvious wealth, had thrown himself into the whole idea of being a countryman, avidly reading anything he could get his hands on which would give him knowledge.

The night before we were to go stalking, as we were by the side of Loch Ness, the conversation had turned to the question of 'The Monster'. I said that I had no hard opinion whether the beast existed or not, stating that from everything I had heard or read I preferred to keep an open mind (and to this day state that I believe it could exist). My host, however, declared his firm belief in its existence, going on to tell us he believed it to be some form of plesiosaur and that it was only a matter of time before its existence was proved. We also mused on how valuable any photographs of the beast would be.

Next morning, after walking a fairly circuitous route due to the wind conditions, we were stalking in on what was a very shootable stag with a party of hinds. I suggested that I lie where I was and that he circled around downhill to put himself in the best possible position for the stag. This required him going some 200 metres or so below me, which would put him well within 80 metres of the stag. He would have the cover of a little hump of ground which he would be to one side of. On the other and out over some rough ground, the stag was grazing. An easy shot and a good stalk.

Eventually he was in position, lying there out of sight of the beast. I, from my higher vantage point, noticed seven equally spaced black dots in the loch, travelling directly in towards the shore below us. Looking through my binoculars I got an excellent view, but in the waves it was difficult to see them all at the same time. They gave the impression that they were undulating. As my friend looked up at me I managed to give him a hand signal and pointed at the loch beyond him. He looked where I was indicating and eventually spotted them whereupon he became highly agitated, but as he raised his binoculars a curtain of mist blew across obscuring the view.

To my astonishment he sprang to his feet. Ignoring the stag he bounded off downhill, running like a hare. The startled deer, seeing him, bounded up hill, stopping some 50 or 60 metres in front of me and looked back. Never one to look a gift horse in the mouth I put the crossed reticules of my scope on the base of his neck and squeezed the trigger. The stag collapsed, dead instantly as the rest of the party sped off. I must say as I gralloched the beast I found myself so amused that I was actually laughing. I mused on my friend's embarrassment when he eventually got to the lochside to get his expected photograph of 'The Monster'. What he would see was seven deer swimming in the loch.

On the high tops stalkers often witness the invincible golden eagle being harried by hooded crows.

Red deer (*Cervus elaphus*)

The male is known as a stag, the female as a hind and the young as a calf.

The red deer is found in most countries in Europe as well as in the Middle East. Its size is governed by its environment. Some of the animals in Yugoslavia and Hungary grow to enormous size, almost twice the weight and antler growth of their Scottish cousins.

The red deer is the largest deer found in Britain, in the counties of Devon and Somerset, Hampshire, Sussex, Staffordshire and Cumbria. In Scotland they may be found in Kircudbrightshire, Ayrshire, and in all the counties north of a line drawn from just north of Glasgow, running above Stirling and across to Perth and Forfar, including the islands of the west coast that are large enough to support them. A few herds occur in the Wicklow mountains of Ireland.

The red deer of Britain can be separated into two different groups – the English and the Scottish. The English deer are generally heavier and with better antler growth as a result of the milder temperature, the lusher feed and the proximity of woodland, although they should not be confused with the park-fed deer of England which are semi-domesticated. The Scottish deer live mainly in the mountain areas of Scotland, and are generally smaller with less antler weight.

It was not always the case. The Scottish red deer up to Victorian times certainly had better quality antlers, there being much less pressure on the deer. Before Queen Victoria started the fashion amongst the English for ownership of a Scottish highland estate, the deer had mainly been taken as food. Some individuals did enjoy hunting deer, but firearms were not as efficient, nor were the hunters as numerous as they are today, and real pressure did not come on deer until the twentieth century. With the increasing number of individuals wishing to shoot deer and the improvement in firearm technology, the numbers of deer shot continued to increase. These shooters were intent on getting the largest set of antlers they could, so the best specimens were always the first to go and inevitably the quality of the deer fell away.

One needs only to go into somewhere like the ballroom at Mar Lodge, Braemar, where there are over 3,000 sets of antlers on the walls and ceiling, to see the superb quality that the deer heads once were. Landseer, the famous artist of the day, whilst no doubt romanticizing some of his game, did accurately reflect the size of the deer that he saw when he was a guest of Queen Victoria, recording with his drawings heads of such a size that today would almost certainly have come from a park.

The average mature highland stag weighs between 89 and 101 kg, although weights do reach up to 125 kg. These heavier beasts are exceptional. A stag, when full grown, stands 100–115 cm at the shoulder. Hinds weigh beween 50 and 70 kg and stand between 95 and 105 cm at the shoulder. These are not, however, the true weights as deer are normally weighed after the beast has been cleaned, its lungs, intestines, stomach and bowels removed, leaving heart, liver and kidneys, i.e. edible offal, in the carcass.

Red deer tracks are fairly short in proportion to their width – 7–8 cm in length and 6–7 cm in width. They are rounded, with deep ridging around the perimeter of both toes. The toes will splay on soft ground, although the ground would have to be exceptionally soft or snow-covered before you could see the dew claws. Red deer gait comprises walk, trot, canter and gallop;

Red stag.

when galloping you would find their slot marks on the ground in
groups of four, 2–3 metres apart.

Stags' droppings during the latter part of the summer, August–
September, and the early part of rut may become much softer in
texture, reflecting the stag's rich, prime condition – he is at his
optimum weight for the year and has been grazing on the rich
summer growth. (The same can be seen with horses and other
grazing animals when they over-indulge on rich grasses.) It is

The telescope is still preferred by Highland stalkers for 'glassing the hill'.

most likely the excited condition of the stag at the early part of the rut that contributes to the softening of its droppings at that time and they are deposited as a small pat. For the rest of the year the stag's droppings are about 2 cm long, pointed at one end and flattened at the other. Hinds' droppings are also about 2 cm in length, rounded at one end and often concave at the other. They almost fit together like the sections of an articulated black string and are sometimes found joined together.

Stags' antlers serve two purposes – defence and to denote rank within the herd. The brow, bay and tray tines point forward and up. Therefore in the event of a stag being pursued by a large predator, the stag's natural running position is with his antlers laid back so that any animal that tried to spring onto its back would be likely to impale itself. Equally, in defence against any animal that was cornering the stag, by lowering its head its formidable weaponry all hooks upwards, so that the stag may inflict maximum damage in the action of raising its head. Today, however, in Britain there are no large predators that can threaten deer and the antlers are used only for jousting with each other at the rut.

Antlers are dropped in early spring and start to grow almost immediately, so that by August they have reached their full size. When a young male is in its second year a small knob appears on its head, giving the animal in the north of Britain the name 'knobber'. In the south it would be referred to as a 'pricket'. In its third year the animal grows little antlers and in the north is

A mixed group of stags make their way out to the hill.

Alan painted the picture entitled *Running Before the Storm* after witnessing this sight near Loch Rannoch.

The painting *Hinds on Meal Gordie* wonderfully evokes the chill mountain air.

In this painting Alan depicts the group of stags that frequented the hill above his studio.

referred to as a 'staggie', in the south as a 'brocket'. One would refer to a young male as being a staggie up until he reached five or six years old, depending on his antler growth, since his size and antlers are what would designate him a full-grown stag.

Although called red deer, their colour varies widely so that in one herd you can often see animals that are dun coloured through all the gradations of reddish brown to a very dark colour that at distance could almost appear chocolate. Their winter coats are fairly harsh and thick, and greyish brown/red in colour. In summer the coat, which has a greyish undercoat, is shorter, less harsh to the touch and reddish brown in colour. The stag generally has a dorsal ridge of longer hair which runs up the back of its neck. As the young stag starts to come into rut he develops a mane which each year progressively becomes thicker, moulting out at the change of his coat in spring. As the stag reaches maturity he retains his mane throughout the year, which adds both to his physical appearance and stature within the hierarchy of the herd.

Red deer are highly herd orientated. Hinds spend much of the year in herds that range in size from ten to one hundred. These herds of hinds and calves are matriarchal, there normally being a distinct leading hind, an older beast, with several mature hinds as lieutenants. The stags herd in groups of anything from two or three to up to thirty or more animals of different ages.

During the period of antler growth the stags gravitate to higher ground where the temperature is cooler, and away from the clouds of flies found on the lower ground. As summer ends the stags start to break into smaller parties as they move back towards the hinds. The rut starts properly around mid-September and continues until the end of October, with a few late stags still roaring into November.

In most areas the rut does not get into full swing until the first few nips of early frost, at which point the stags start to cut out a number of hinds for themselves. This is only successfully achieved by mature stags who can fight off lesser stags. A stag will have his hinds, anything in number from two or three to twenty or more, which he will round up and hold together. During this period most of the hinds are happy to graze quietly — not so the stags. Younger beasts constantly try to slip in on the side of the herd and cut out a hind of their own, whilst the stag holding the herd rushes first in one direction and then another, chasing off the younger ambitious stags. After a few days of constant running around his herd, protecting it and serving as

The largest red deer stag the author has shot. A 13-pointer, an old beast past his prime.

many of the hinds as he can, and not taking time to graze, the stag's condition drops dramatically. He loses weight and is referred to as 'run'.

Stags shot during the rut are not as good for the table – the flesh tends to have lost all its fat and has taken on the pungency of the rutting animal. However, the rut is by far the most popular time for stalking. The stags are active as they chase after the hinds and the very essence of the rut, the roar of the stags, makes it such an exciting time on the hill.

Although stags are what people always associate with stalking, this I believe is due to two things, one being, as I have previously said, the excitement of the rut, and the second of course that stags have antlers, a tangible trophy of the chase. Hinds, conversely, are generally regarded as of lesser importance, partly because they lack antlers and partly because of man's instinctive distaste of killing the female. However, proper management dictates that to achieve a good balance, the hinds must also be culled, and it should be said that in general stalking hinds can be

Above Hinds in the snow.

Right A group of stags in the morning sun.

Opposite above Hinds making their way on to the hill.

Opposite below Typical Scottish stalking country.

more difficult than stalking stags. Stags are invariably in much smaller herds, and during the rut have their minds on other things. Hinds, however, are always in larger groups, are generally more alert, and by the simple mathematics of a greater number of animals having a greater number of noses, eyes and ears to spot you, they can be the more challenging stalking.

The rifle calibre I recommend for red deer is .243 or .270.

I have shot many stags. One which comes to mind any time I think of stalking stories was a quite splendid 'royal' with truly fabulous antler growth.

My wife Shena had often listened to various friends talking about occasions when I had called stags during the rut. One particular friend who was visiting us during the stalking season was marvelling, over dinner, about his experiences that day as I called them. Shena suggested I take her out stalking and show her what they were so enthusiastic about. I was of course delighted at this opportunity of showing off my prowess to my wife and the following day we went out on the hill.

It was a perfect day for the rut – crisp, sharp, bright sunlight, a beautiful October morning. We walked out the access track for three or five kilometres, to an area that I knew would hold good beasts. I found myself enjoying the experience more than I ever had with any of my stalking friends. Shena was interested in every aspect of the hill and took great pleasure as I pointed out the different sights – peregrines, an eagle and, of course, the deer of various ages.

We reached the area where I expected to find good stags and true enough, across some flat ground on a ridge were three parties of stags and hinds. One or two other stags on the periphery were trying to capture some hinds of their own. The only approach I could see was across the flat ground using what folds and hollows there were. But eventually, we got ourselves to a situation where it was impossible to go forward and still the nearest deer were about half a kilometre away. I suggested I try calling a stag over, explaining that the note and depth of the call was important. Too deep a call and no right thinking stag would wish to do battle with what might sound like the biggest stag in creation. Too light a call and no self-respecting stag would bother to come looking for a teenager.

Lying together in the heather I started to call, getting an almost immediate answer. For some time I lay roaring at the answering stag. Suddenly he started galloping toward us, stop-

Hooded crows, highland scavengers.

ping at about 100 metres, looking for us and roaring. I roared him on, he galloped another 50 metres and stopped, swishing his antlers and roaring. I coughed a few hoarse grunts, and the stag, like a trotting horse, lifting his feet high in the air, came prancing forward, grunting and roaring, while I egged him on. Eventually he was no more than 7 or 8 metres from us, his great nostrils searching the air which told him nothing. The light breeze was blowing straight towards us.

He really was an awesome sight, a magnificent mature royal, looking both majestic and frightening. Suddenly he turned and ran back to about 30 metres. We both started to breathe again. I gave a couple of grunts and in his high stepping fashion he came straight back to us. When he was about 4 metres from us I was sure he would keep coming and certainly did not want to risk any mishap, so I stood up. For what seemed like several seconds, but was probably not, the stag looked at me, then he turned and galloped off.

An unseen young stag will soon announce the stalker's presence.

This was the sort of day on the hill that gives deer stalking its magic. The stag coming as close as he did, something I had never experienced before, made it even more special.

EUROPEAN GAME

If it is your intention to visit Europe to shoot game, you will find many species which also occur in Britain. However, in addition there are bear, bison, wolf, lynx, boar, mouflon and chamois. It is not my intention to cover the first four of these species, since shooting them is rare and particularly expensive. I will instead concentrate on the more common species that most people would be attracted to shoot.

If you wish to shoot boar, chamois or mouflon, this will obviously entail a journey to the Continent. Almost certainly you will make your booking through one of the many sporting agencies specializing in Europe, including the Eastern Bloc. They are the only people who know intimately what is available, and although they are commercial enterprises and must make a profit, resulting in your shooting costing you a bit more, I thoroughly recommend booking through an agency as it is the only good guide to what you might expect. With the multiple problems you may encounter with local gun laws, importation permits, game licences, calibre restrictions, language, etc., it does make sense to use them. The only safe alternative is for you to have your booking made by a friend in the country you intend to visit.

Elk (*Alces alces*)

The male is known as a bull, the female as a cow and the young as a calf.

A close cousin of the moose of North America, the elk is the largest species of deer to be found in Europe. A very large animal, a big bull weighs up to 500 kg and stands 180–185 cm at the shoulder. With its distinctive appearance, elk cannot be mistaken for any other species. It has long legs and a large long head with an overhanging muzzle. Compared with other species of deer, the neck of the elk is regarded as fairly short; it also has a hanging dewlap, referred to as a bell. The most distinguishing feature of the elk is its palmated antlers which, on a European head, could have a spread of 120 cm, with 16 to 20 points.

In its summer coat the elk is a brownish grey, with greyish legs of a paler tone — though colour variation can be considerable, with some animals having an overall greyer tinge, while others can be particularly dark. Its winter coat, which tends to be lighter in colour than the summer coat, is denser and longer.

The habitat that elk prefer is woodland. Indeed, elk cannot survive without a woodland environment with plenty of wet areas, bogland and lake surrounds, to provide the aquatic plants that form part of their diet, particularly during the three summer months of June, July and August. Other foods eaten are a wide variety of bulbs, shoots, shrubs, leaves and grasses.

The elk is particularly numerous in parts of wooded Scandinavia, Norway, Sweden and Finland, and is found right across parts

The European elk, with its palmated antlers, is highly distinctive.

of northern Europe to the east of the Urals. Elk were found in Britain until around the ninth century and it is likely that their extinction in Britain is principally attributable to the gradual destruction of the forest habitat they required.

The rut lasts from mid-September until mid-October and it is only during this period that the normally silent bull can be heard making a sound, a deep grunt which does not travel. The cow uses her voice throughout the year – a nasal sound – though normally only when calling to her calf.

Due to the habitat that elk favour and the fact that the principal predators of the species are bears or packs of wolves, they are numerous and shooting them tends to be less selective than species that frequent more open spaces. There are areas where elk are stalked in a similar way to the stalking that the British sportsman is familiar with, but because of the density and scale of their range, they tend to be driven. The normal elk shooting exercise is that the sportsmen, several in number, are given a clearing or ride to cover, while an area is driven by the locally preferred dogs, such as elk hounds.

A typical scenario would be the sportsman standing quietly

in the chill northern weather, listening and watching. If he were lucky, he would hear the dogs approaching, though often there is little warning before the elk appear, when the sportsman must make a speedy assessment of the age, size and quality of the animal, and then make a quick and accurate shot. Due to its enormous size, it is necessary to employ teamwork to drag the carcass out, and the whole party would normally become involved in the removal of the carcass.

The rifle calibre I recommend is .30–06 180 gr. or Win. Mag. 180 gr.

Personally, I do not find elk shooting particularly thrilling, since I prefer stalking. However, it does have great attraction if you are lucky to have the combination of good weather and good stance where you can enjoy the environment and watching the wildlife, although it is necessary never to lose concentration, for the instant you do is the moment that some wonderful big old bull crosses your sights! It is also most important that you are highly confident in your abilities to lift your rifle, swing and fire with a high degree of accuracy.

Mouflon (*Ovis musimon*)

The male is known as a ram, the female as a ewe and the young as a lamb.

To describe the mouflon as a wild sheep is akin to describing the Cape buffalo as a wild cow, for as much as the Cape buffalo resembles a Jersey does the mouflon resemble a Cheviot. Originating in Sardinia and Corsica, the mouflon has been introduced as a sporting animal throughout Europe and can be found in France, Cyprus, Turkey, Sardinia and Czechoslovakia where the majority of record mouflon have been shot.

Although mouflon are natural inhabitants of high mountain ranges, they do, however, enjoy the environment of the European forests, particularly deciduous areas, and can provide most exciting stalking. In winter mouflon have a thick dense coat of chestnut brown, with a distinct black throat ruff or mane, although colour variations of browns ranging from deep to almost gold are found in different locales. Mature animals, particularly the older rams, develop a light coloured saddle patch. With their almost black mane, chest and flanks and white muzzle, belly, lower legs and rump, they are quite magnificent-looking animals. Their summer coats, when moulted out to the lighter summer weight, have a general overall lighter, brighter appearance. The ewes or females are normally hornless although small horns do occasionally appear. The rams have heavily corrugated horns which grow in a spiral.

The mouflon rut is normally during November and December, with the ewes dropping one or two lambs in April or May.

The recommended rifle calibre for mouflon, .243 with 100 gr. ammunition, is certainly perfectly capable of dealing with the mouflon and has a flatter trajectory at longer range than a .30–06 180 gr. which have greater knock-down power. A more suitable alternative for those wanting a cartridge combining flat trajectory with greater knock-down power would be the .300 Win. Mag 180 gr.

I was invited to Czechoslovakia as a guest of some Italian friends, who met me at the airport. We drove to the hunting area, which they had rented for two weeks' mixed stalking. They had already been there for a week and from their description had had a quite wonderful time. Game was in abundance and Giorgio, my host, told me that the only animal that had eluded them was a trophy mouflon. They had just not managed to get closer than an occasional glimpse of the mouflon in the distance, and then they had not managed to spot any good rams.

Next day, to give myself time to get acclimatized, it was suggested that I stay behind and stalk some lower slopes with the under gamekeeper, whilst Giorgio and the headkeeper went to the higher ground where they expected to find mouflon. At first light I set out with the young man, who spoke sufficient English for us to make ourselves understood, to look for a really nice roe. However, as we set out I glassed the rocks above the area we were going to stalk, and the first animal I spotted was a mouflon ewe, then another and another. As we lay watching, a quite magnificent ram appeared. The young gamekeeper became highly excited. This, he explained, was a wonderful beast and was meant for me. So we set off on a circular route that would bring us with luck, above where the animals were.

Eventually I found myself lying on a knoll, looking down at the mouflon which were grazing along the hillside. We stalked them, the stalk lasting for a good two hours, before I judged that I was close enough, about 90 metres, to take a shot. I had to take a sitting shot. I held my reticules on his shoulder, debating with

A mouflon ram.

myself whether to shoot him in the heart, when he raised his head and turned broadside. I moved the cross on to the base of his neck and fired. He dropped, rolled over and lay still. I had just shot, the keeper told me, a superior mouflon and it had been an exciting stalk.

That evening when Giorgio returned he was excited – he had finally stalked and shot a good ram and insisted we go immediately to the larder where I could inspect it. When we got there the keeper had hung it beside mine. The expression on Giorgio's face was hilarious as he looked at his and then at mine. I couldn't resist smiling as I congratulated him on shooting the smaller cousin of mine.

Chamois (*Rupicapra rupicapra*)

The male is known as a billy, the female as a nanny and the young as a kid.

I believe part of the attraction of stalking chamois is the magnificent countryside which you invariably find at the heights that these wild goats are to be discovered. It is also a testament to your fitness that you can get amongst the chamois for they inhabit the high mountains of the Alps!

Stalking chamois initially entails a long uphill climb early in the morning, so that by first light you are high in the range and ready to start spotting for suitable animals. It is quite common on arrival at some vantage point with your alpenjaeger to sit down to await the sun burning off the surrounding mists — as it does so some spectacular vista below you is revealed as you realize how high you have climbed. Once chamois have been spotted and the decision made which one to stalk, the stalk is no different from any other high ground stalk. However, due to the barrenness of some of the high tops there is little cover for the stalker. In addition, you are sometimes compelled to shoot across a gully so you can expect to shoot at fairly long range.

The recommended calibre, .243 with 100 gr. ammunition, is certainly perfectly capable of dealing with the chamois. A more suitable alternative for those wanting a cartridge combining flat trajectory with greater knock-down power would be the .300 Win. Mag 180 gr.

I had been getting myself fit for the coming trip to shoot chamois and was greatly looking forward to the trip to Austria. It was dark when I arrived at the estate and quickly unpacked and went down to join my host to a really splendid alpine dinner.

Next morning, feeling slightly hung over, I stood in the kitchen swallowing strong Continental coffee and eating crois-sants. Then there was a tap at the door. The jaeger, Eckart, had arrived and after introductions we set off in the darkness. Eckart knew where we were going. He led, my host second and myself third. We tramped on, at first through gentle alpine meadows, always upward. Then the ground became steeper, and on we walked. Apart from occasional breathing stops, which Eckart allowed my host and myself, there was no conversation, nor delays.

After walking uphill for at least two hours we sat down. It was beginning to lighten, but we were in an area of thick mist.

The photograph (*left*) shows clearly the goat eye that gives the chamois its excellent sight. Alan took the photograph while stalking chamois and researching for his delightful painting (*below*).

Visibility was not more than a few metres. My host drew his loden cloak around him, put Eckart's haversack under his head and promptly went to sleep. Eckart and I sat quietly, waiting for the mist to clear. I had no idea where we were, only that we had been walking upwards for some time. Suddenly the sun came out. The mists melted away and I was faced with the most breathtaking view right in front of me. We were on top of a mountain, looking down to the alpine valley far below.

I gave my host a nudge, he awakened and we started to carefully glass the area in front of us. We could see no chamois and so began walking along the side of the mountain. We had walked on more than a kilometre until we came to a tight fold in the hillside running above us and there up on the face was a small group of chamois. Eckart worked out the stalk. I was pleased, when he started to tell us his intentions, that I had worked out the same stalking route.

It was decided that the three of us should stalk together. We slowly made our way uphill until at last Eckart signalled that he thought we should take a shot. My host indicated I should go first. Eckart indicated the particular animal that he preferred I shoot. The range was about 100 metres. I lay down, took careful aim and shot the beast in the shoulder.

Almost on the report of my rifle, my host fired at his chamois. As the rest of the group of animals ran off, we congratulated each other. Two shots, two chamois.

European wild boar (*Sus scrofa*)

The male is known as a boar, the female as a sow and the young as a piglet.

The European wild boar ranges from France to the USSR, and from northern Europe down through Italy and North Africa. They have been part of the hunting tradition of Europe since earliest times, and are an integral part of forest areas right across Europe.

The British sportsman who wishes to shoot boar has a wide choice of locales with an equally wide range of standards and prices, up to French châteaux with superior cuisine, great traditions, and everything designed to enhance the sport. Poland, which has the largest boar but has limitations like the rest of the Eastern Bloc regarding accommodation, has much to commend it. Tunisian boar shooting is less expensive than in Europe but the standard of accommodation and amenities available to the sportsman is basic.

Depending on the area, boar are shot either with a rifle or shotgun loaded with Brenica slug. In Tunisia, for example, rifles are not allowed and it is shotgun only. If boar are being driven, they are normally intercepted by the guns that have been placed in rides, some of them quite narrow, and a high degree of speed shooting will be required. Boar run at quite some speed and the inexperienced never fail to be surprised. Because of their large size, it is easy to get the idea that they will somehow be a slower moving target. Not so. They are an extremely fast and highly exciting sporting animal. It is, however, essential that you shoot them in the shoulder/chest area since it is desirable that they do not go on into the thicket wounded. Apart from the distasteful thought of wounded game, retrieving a wounded boar is not for the faint-hearted.

One alternative to driven boar is to shoot them from a high seat. In some areas it is possible for stalkers who wish to go after a large trophy boar individually to stalk the beast accompanied by only one keeper. For those who are superior stalkers able to slip silently through the woods this can be highly exciting.

Where possible, if you are taking your own rifle to shoot boar abroad, I would recommend .30–06 with 180 gr. ammunition. For a shotgun, use Brenica slug.

I have never been particularly attracted to the idea of shooting animals from a high seat. Whilst it is necessary to use high seats in certain forest areas, it is to me not much more exhiliarating than going to a fairground shooting gallery. All one needs is a degree of luck, the ability to sit still and the skill to shoot accurately.

For me the prospect of shooting driven boar was exciting. The only downside was that I had to give a commentary as I did it, in the filming of *Wild Boar Shooting*.

We flew to Tunisia, drove into the mountain area near An Drahan and started all the background filming that would be necessary to make the programme. Eventually we were taken to the area where we would be shooting — mountains covered with cork oak and small firs, interlaced with narrow rides. We set up the cameras and the *rabateurs* (beaters) started driving the blocks of timber. Jackals and foxes appeared, slipping silently across the rides. A red deer, so rare in Tunisia that they enjoy nationwide protection, came out of the thicket beside me.

Then the first boar appeared. They shot across the ride with such speed that I instinctively knew the cameraman would be having nightmares trying to focus on their dashing bodies. Then out came a big boar, almost at my leg. As he dashed across the narrow ride I swung through and fired, striking him perfectly behind the shoulder. He literally flew on into the undergrowth, dead in the air. He was a silver medal boar, an excellent trophy to have shot, particularly on film.

But when we examined the film we realized that the rides were so narrow and the boar crossed them so quickly that it was over before the viewer would have registered the boar. Also, unless I managed to kill one in the middle of the ride it might appear that it ran on wounded. Even the one we had on film, when shown at normal speed, seemed to jump into the undergrowth. Only when we slowed the film down could you clearly see that it was struck in mid-stride and had been killed.

I explained our problem to our Tunisian guide. We had to have an open area. He was not hopeful and we spent several days

Wild boar in a wallow.

The author with two magnificent boar, one silver medal, one gold medal.

fruitlessly setting up the camera and driving blocks of woodland, which held nothing more exciting than a few jackals. Then on the last day we had to film we went to a mountain area where I was introduced to the head man of the village, a little man with a wispy beard, a long coat, wellington boots with holes and a turban, with a hunting horn hanging on string around his neck. I got a different feeling. I recognized in the old man an authority absent in the others. His attitude to me was noble, not the feeling of servility backed by need for our money which I experienced from the others.

We set off and after about an hour he indicated a broad clearing on top of a hill, pointing where he thought I should stand and where we should position the camera. I stood under a cork oak as I heard the beaters far down the slope start the drive. The sun lit the area in front of me, which almost seemed like a stage set. Even the trees were prettier here. It is difficult to describe the feeling of knowing that everything was right, but I did. I looked up at the camera crew, some 60 metres away and silently signalled that they should get ready. This was it.

Fifteen minutes later the dogs started frantically yapping. They were coming in my direction. I looked down the slope behind me — thick shrubbery everywhere. The yapping got louder. Then into a clearing below me ran a huge boar. He was bigger than anything I had seen. As he trotted along he swung his great head from side to side, grunting, almost asking the pack at his heels to come up to the front where his huge white gleaming tusks could deal with them. I signalled to the camera to turn over. I looked back at the boar. He was 5 metres behind me. Then suddenly he broke into the clearing. As I started to lift my gun, he saw the movement and accelerated. I swung through, and fired. The slug struck him perfectly in the base of the neck. He somersaulted and lay still as the pack of small dogs surrounded him.

I looked up at the camera crew. I could see the cameraman with his eye to the viewer, still intently filming the dogs surrounding the boar. Then he switched off the camera and took his eye from the viewer. He looked at me with an enormous grin as he gave me the thumbs up sign. What we had on film was a unique sequence of a gold medal boar running out in perfect focus, in perfect light, in ideal surroundings and the shot, too, when it came, was perfect.

CHAPTER SIX

Feathered Game

TYPES OF SHOOT

There are three types of shooting where birds are shot with a shotgun – rough shooting, flighting and driven. Rough shooting is a casual, low-key affair where the sportsman, referred to as 'the gun', either on his own or in the company of a friend, works the dogs down a hedgerow, through some cover or along a reeded ditch. The intention is to flush any lurking game in front of the dog, giving the gun an opportunity for a sporting shot. Walked up game can be quite the most pleasant shooting activity. The emphasis is on the gun enjoying the various aspects of the occasion — working his dog, the excitement of flushing game, and if in company, the companionship of a friend. The emphasis is not on bagging large numbers of birds. Indeed, a couple of rabbits, perhaps a cock pheasant and a duck or two – what would be referred to as a good mixed bag – and most sportsmen would regard such a walked up day as having been successful. Many of my own happiest shooting occasions over the years have been by myself with my dog working a patch of cover to flush a hoped-for lurking bird. It would be fair to say that there are few sportsmen who would not, if asked, state that some of the shooting they have most enjoyed was a day's rough shooting.

Flighting can be pigeon shooting over decoys during the day or as they go in to evening roost, wildfowling on the foreshore in the early dawn, or shooting geese inland over decoys or duck as they come in to their chosen pond in the dusk. Flighting can be highly exciting, although with the exception of pigeon on a warm day, most flighting entails a degree of discomfort, often with wet and cold for good measure, with the occasional highlights of a few birds presenting themselves as a challenging shot for the gun. But such is the magic of flighting that although it is not to everyone's taste, to those whom the bug has bitten, flighting can be most exciting. With the exception of pigeon, where large bags are acceptable, most forms of flighting would be self-limiting; for instance, it would be unlikely on the foreshore for multiple opportunities to be presented to the gun, all of which he successfully shot. In situations where large bags could be achieved — geese in certain conditions, early season duck — if the gun had any sporting integrity at all, he would limit himself in the number of birds he shot.

A driven day, if properly conducted, is without doubt the most exciting form of shooting. Refined over the years as a 'gentleman's' sport, each aspect of the day is geared to give the guns maximum sport with minimum discomfort. It is also the one form of shooting where great emphasis is placed on the presentation of the birds, that is the way in which the host or gamekeeper has laid out the shooting, using the topography — hilltops, banks, high trees — to make the birds as difficult and challenging as possible.

With grouse, for example, well positioned butts are those placed where neither the guns nor the birds get too long to see each other, since the birds would veer away from the line of guns, and the guns, if watching birds coming from a long way, would be more likely to poke as opposed to swing through. The same would apply with partridges, the host placing the guns in the best positions to achieve both surprise to the birds and sport to the guns.

Again, with pheasants, since they are birds which inhabit a more wooded environment, lines of high trees and slopes can be used to make the birds fly high — and a high curving pheasant presents a highly challenging target. (No gun would want to shoot what may be referred to as an easy target in which there is neither sport nor pleasure.) For example, this can be achieved where the birds are driven out of cover on the top of a bank or slope towards a line of beech trees. These would make the birds fly up and over. The guns, positioned some 60 metres behind the beeches, would then get a presentation of birds which would be highly sporting.

With driven birds there is much greater emphasis on numbers. To make the day a success there would have to be, let us say, eight or ten guns, and if each gun were to shoot only twenty birds, that would account for 200 birds. It would be unrealistic to expect the wild population of either partridge or pheasant to be able to sustain this number of birds shot annually nationwide. They are therefore bred, distributed and regarded as a crop by the estates where driven shooting is practised. Indeed, these birds when released top up the wild population if they can avoid the guns.

Grouse are reluctant to breed in captivity and it has been found that the only way successful populations can be reared is with proper moor management. This of course creates a degree of exclusivity with the grouse, unlike the easily bred partridge and pheasant. Grouse shooting is therefore by necessity more expensive.

A pair of capercaillie in the branches of a Scots pine.

Indeed, any form of driven shooting is expensive to lay on, with the costs of beaters, pickers-up and the breeding of birds all amounting to substantial sums. It has therefore always been regarded as an exclusive sport, confined to those who can afford it.

GAME BIRDS

Capercaillie (*Tetrao urogallus*)

The capercaillie is the largest of the game birds in the British Isles, though as a result of its extinction as a British species it was not designated a game bird in the Game Act of 1831. Later in the 1830s the introduction of Swedish birds to a Perthshire estate started the re-establishment of the capercaillie in Scotland. Capercaillie are found in Scandinavia, the Alps and Pyrenees, northern Europe, Yugoslavia, Poland, Russia – in fact almost anywhere in northern Europe where pine forests are found – but in Britain it is now found only in Scotland, in areas around Loch Lomond, central Perthshire, and throughout parts of eastern Scotland in a triangle from Perth to Banff to Dingwall. There are also other areas on the periphery of this range where pockets of capercaillie thrive.

The capercaillie is to my eye a quite awesome bird and to describe it as a large grouse is slightly misleading, for whilst that is what it is, it really is huge, more the size of a turkey. At first the cock bird appears to be black, but his plumage, when examined, shows that the breast has a dark bottle green tinge. His primaries have brown/grey tinges and he has a marked red wattle over the eye. The plumage under the cock bird's bill hangs at a steep angle and gives the impression that the cock has a great beard. Hen birds are smaller, with a brown mottled coloration, and a reddish patch on the breast. Both birds have feathered legs.

Cock birds can weigh from 3,400 to 4,500 g, with an average cock weighing 4,000 g. Some specimens are claimed to have weighed as much as 8,000 g. Hen birds weigh from 1,500 to 2,000 g, with an average weight of 1,800 g. Some specimens can weigh as much as 2,600 g.

Cock capercaillie during the breeding season become very

protective of their territory. They will quite readily attack a human intruder if he is in the wrong place at the wrong time. An example of this behaviour was observed on a small golf course near my home. A large cock bird took up residence in some woods around the 8th hole and would happily come out threatening any golfer who came into the vicinity. Such attacks are not serious. They are posturing with wings hooded and tail spread. It is at this time that the normally quiet cock bird becomes very vocal, giving out a whole series of gobbling and grinding sounds which at first hearing do not seem possibly to come from a bird. Hen birds tend to restrict their vocal activity to a variety of low croaking sounds.

The habitat that the capercaillie depends on is the very reason why the bird would be unlikely ever to spread much beyond its current range. It favours the large traditional pine forests typified by the old Caledonian Forest. Modern forestry plantations of tightly packed commercially grown firs with no planned open areas are not attractive to wildlife and the capercaillie is no exception. Its ideal environment can be seen in the areas around Mar, in any of the Spey/Dee valleys, or on any hillside well-grown with Scots pine with lots of open areas.

Capercaillie will live in other coniferous woodland and in areas in Perthshire they have taken residence in some of the more mature commercial forests. In these areas there is little disturbance and the birds have done well. Capercaillie will also live in mixed coniferous/deciduous woodland. A good example of this was several islands on Loch Lomond where capercaillie took up residence, although as disturbances from weekend boating/fishing increased, numbers reduced.

The capercaillie's preference for Scots-pine forests is clearly due to its dependency on the Scots pine for food. The bird also eats both larch and Douglas fir. A high percentage of the bird's food is the needles of the tree, but of course the bird also eats the new growth, shoots and the cones. In addition to its preference for a restricted range of conifers, the capercaillie will eat other foods, particularly during the spring and summer, a period which, in the north of Scotland, Scandinavia and the high tundra of Alaska, is rich in new growth. Leaves, buds, berries and fruits are in abundance and the capercaillie includes them in its diet, as it will insects, beetles and worms.

Indeed, it is due to its diet being largely pine orientated that the capercaillie has the reputation of tasting of turpentine. There are, however, several different recipes where this taste can be disguised and I personally have found capercaillie most acceptable on the table.

Due to the density of the forest areas of Scandinavia, capercaillie there are normally shot with a shotgun by someone alone who has managed to put one up, or often with a rifle after they have been seen sitting in a prominent position. They are not normally driven to guns in countries other than Britain.

If driven they are wonderful sporting birds, making for fast difficult shooting in spite of their large size. They fly in the same style as grouse or partridge with a series of fast wing beats followed by long glides on bowed wings. It should be said, however, that shooting capercaillie should be strictly limited to estates that have an abundance of the birds and where cropping is therefore ecologically acceptable. The temptation to shoot a capercaillie should never be yielded to unless the gun knows that the bird is numerous in that particular area.

The recommended shot size for the capercaillie is 3 or 4.

Black grouse (*Lyrurus tetrix*)

Whilst the black grouse is normally perceived to be a bird of Scotland and Scandinavia, it is in fact a bird which is still found in parts of England and Wales. At one time the black grouse was much more widely spread throughout England than it is now, but due to the changing agricultural picture in England and increased disturbance, the bird's range has reduced dramatically.

Today in Britain a few pairs live on Exmoor, but generally the black grouse is found in the north of England in a few localized areas, and in larger numbers in the Lake District. The bird is fairly common in parts of Wales, but its real British stronghold is in Scotland where it is found in most areas, with the exception of the high western mountains.

The male black grouse — known as a blackcock — is a most attractive bird. It has a highly distinctive lyre-shaped tail with the most striking glossy blue-black plumage, and a bright red wattle which is particularly prominent in the breeding season. The blackcock has a small white shoulder patch and white undertail coverts. This striking bird is not quite so smart during the autumn when the plumage takes on a distinctly dull appearance.

The hen black grouse is known as a greyhen and can easily be confused with hen capercaillie or red grouse. In common with most female game birds, the greyhen is camouflaged by her

Blackcock at the lek, intent on little else but their ritual performance.

plumage so that she can blend into her habitat, particularly when nesting. She is a reddish rust colour, often with coppery flecks. She has a brown tail, neck and head, with fine black barring. If seen together with the red grouse and capercaillie, the colour differentials are more easily seen, and the greyhen is obviously larger with a distinct grey tinge which is absent on the red grouse. Apart from being smaller than the hen capercaillie the greyhen has considerably less barring. The greyhen also has a forked tail.

Blackcock range in weight, depending on food and area, from 1,000 to 1,700 g, a good average weight being 1,250 g. The greyhen has a weight range of between 800 and 1,200 g, with an average of 900 g.

Blackcock are normally quiet, but in the run up to and during the lek they make a 'coo-coo-ing' sound, not dissimilar to roosting pigeons though the blackcock is more gutteral. The greyhen makes a sound similar to the 'kok-kok-kok' of the pheasant.

The black grouse lek is probably the most well-known of all game birds' breeding displays and this unusual habit is well documented in both photographs and art. Leks are traditionally held on the same spot every year, cock birds starting to congregate in March. Numbers of birds at the leks vary – one beside my house will normally have from five to seven cocks, though I have seen other leks where fourteen cocks regularly gathered.

The lek displays occur at dawn and will last two or three hours and often for an hour or so in the evening. This display can take place over a period of four to six weeks, building up from a few early arrivals to a peak when the lek is in full swing. The lek is really just a series of displays and posturing; no real fighting or damage takes place. Some fights can appear to be more serious but the norm would be that cocks, with wings open and tails spread, do a series of hopping dances. The greyhens arrive at the leks anything from two to four weeks after the lek has started. Often greyhens may well display to each other. Their selection made, the birds mate.

During the period of the lek, the birds appear to be at times so intent on the ceremony that they are oblivious to other happenings. This was well illustrated when a friend and myself were watching a lek. We had lain for some time, hidden, when we both witnessed a peregrine strike a lapwing, which fell fairly close to the blackcock. The peregrine followed the lapwing down and proceeded to pluck and eat it, all the while being ignored by the posturing blackcock.

Black grouse are found in a greater mix of territory than either the red grouse or capercaillie. The country it seems to prefer is heather moorland, fringed with mature conifers, with a boggy wetland. The bird will then move happily between all three. Black grouse, however, will also happily live in birch woodland and many of the higher birch plantations seem to hold black grouse. On some of the lower ground – in central Perthshire, for example, where the countryside is a mix of arable fields, fringed fairly thickly with trees with good undergrowth – you will often see black grouse, particularly during autumn, as they move freely from stubble into the cover of the trees.

It is predominantly due to the black grouse's longer dietary list that the bird has a greater range than the red grouse or capercaillie. As with the red grouse, heather is an important staple in their diet, but they will eat a greater variety of foods, including moorland berries, seeds, shoots and buds. During late summer and autumn they will happily feed on grain, seeds, flowers, grasses, berries and insects, and will also eat potatoes and other root vegetables.

Due to the density of the forest areas of Scandinavia, as with capercaillie, black grouse are usually taken with a shotgun by someone alone, who has managed to put one up, or with a rifle if they have been seen sitting in a prominent position. And as with capercaillie, they are not normally driven to guns in countries other than Britain.

Black grouse can be quite exhilarating sport and when driven will often present harder targets than red grouse. They have the same flight pattern as the other game birds — fast wing beats alternating with gliding. The black grouse can reach speeds which are certainly faster than red grouse. They also have the sporting advantage in that they are normally driven from woodland and give the guns less warning of their arrival. Of the many game birds that I have shot, prominent amongst my most exciting experiences are driven blackcock.

The recommended shot size for black grouse is 5 or 6.

Red grouse (*Lagopus lagopus*)

The red grouse is undoubtedly regarded as the king of game birds. This is as much due to the money which is commanded for shooting red grouse as to the sporting nature of the bird. As the cost of shooting red grouse has escalated the more exalted the position of the bird has become in the sportsman's eye. Annually large numbers of wealthy people from around the world journey to Britain to shoot the grouse and a modern tradition reflective of stately living has been built around the traditional grouse shooting season.

The grouse has many attributes. If the moor is well run and the grouse stocks healthy then the birds can be numerous, giving good bags. The moors are almost always in areas of scenic beauty. Shooting grouse commands high money, so with the combination of good bags, beautiful countryside, traditional country-house luxury and exclusivity, it is highly desirable.

Grouse stocks have dramatically decreased in some areas in recent years with a resultant economic squeeze, particularly in Scotland, and much research has gone in to why this has occurred. It would be wrong to lay the blame for the grouse decrease on any one cause, and indeed several factors have contributed in some areas.

One major cause is that the grouse is host to internal parasites, a group of thread worms called *Strongylus*, which bring grouse disease. Another reason for the decline in grouse numbers is a combination of over-shooting and poor management. With the

Red grouse abound near
Alan's studio.

increase of shooting let by the week and the need to offer up
grouse to high-paying guns at all costs, estate managements
have put the game under increasing pressure. This has been
coupled with a decline in the numbers of gamekeepers so that the
moors have been less carefully managed. The result is that grouse
numbers have decreased.

The red grouse is found throughout the Scottish highlands and
islands and in much of the lowland hills. In England it is found on
the Yorkshire moors, parts of the Lake District and the Pennines.
Wales has some good moors. There are small numbers of birds
on Exmoor and Dartmoor. In Ireland the bird is well spread on
appropriate moors throughout the country.

The male grouse is in his smartest plumage during summer
when he is quite resplendent. His eyebrow is bright red and
large. His plumage is a dark reddish brown colour, although the
colour does have a wide variation depending on the area in
which he lives. Some birds in Perthshire, for instance, are
markedly darker than birds in Aberdeenshire. Irish birds are not
as strongly coloured as their Scottish counterparts.

Hen grouse are generally duller, their plumage having more brown and buff or yellow mottles. Both sexes in winter plumage have white underwing markings and a general overall grey appearance.

Cock grouse weigh from 600 to 700 g, the average being 650 g. Hen grouse weigh from 540 to 660 g with an average of 600 g.

There are two sounds evocative of wild moorland: the cry of the curlew and the 'go-back, go-back, go-back' of the red grouse. The cock also make another noise — 'kok...kok...ok...ok'. The hen restricts her sounds to low croaks.

The red grouse lives almost the whole year entirely dependent on rough ling heather. It provides the birds with shelter and sustenance and there are no moors with healthy grouse stocks that do not have heather. Indeed, it is one of the problems that inhibits the successful breeding of grouse in captivity. They eat the shoots, flowers and seed heads of the heather. They also eat the flowers and shoots of all the other vegetation that grows in their environment; the shoots and fruits of bilberries, cranberries

This painting of a hill fox is entitled *A Narrow Escape*, referring to the grouse feathers in front of the fox — left by the fleeing bird.

and virtually all the grasses and plants that grow on the hill.

Visitors to well-managed grouse moors are often surprised to see small piles of grit deposited at the sides of hill tracks, and the natural assumption is that they are there to grit the track. Indeed, the piles of grit are for the grouse, dropped off by the keepers, as grit is essential for the bird's digestion. Although it is normally plentiful, in some areas it needs to be supplemented by the gamekeeper.

An interesting behavioural trait of the red grouse is that if chased away from its range by either beating, driving sheep, or general disturbance by hill walkers, it will return to its own patch time and again.

To take part in a day's driven grouse shooting is certainly to enjoy what must surely be one of the great sporting experiences. The birds fly in typical game bird fashion, with quick beats followed by gliding, and if the butts are carefully positioned, the birds approach the guns without undue warning, to present the guns with the most testing targets. They can be truly sporting birds.

The recommended shot size for red grouse is 6 or 7.

Ptarmigan (*Lagopus mutus*)

Few British sportsmen are ever in a position to see a ptarmigan, far less to shoot one, since these birds have a restricted range in the high mountains of Scotland. Since in the main they live at the top of mountain ranges, the only people who are likely ever to see them are hill climbers, shepherds and stalkers.

The ptarmigan is the game bird of the high regions of mountain areas and is found in Scandinavia, North America and Iceland, and in Asia and the Alps. In Scotland it is found in Stirlingshire, Cape Wrath, several areas of Perthshire and up through the Grampians.

Since the ptarmigan lives in an area without trees and the habitat is either rock, heather or snow, it has evolved the most effective camouflage. Ptarmigan are camouflaged throughout the year, and their spring and summer plumage disguises them wonderfully in both heather and scree. One must remember that the bird developed this disguise as much to hide from the keen eye of both eagle and peregrine as the fox.

During summer they are often confused with grouse as their plumage is similar. Male birds are a dark brown/grey, with the female being a buff colour, barred with reddish brown. During the latter half of the summer, from August, both birds take on a greyer colouring. The cock birds are lighter grey, but the hen has obvious greyer tinges. It is during the early winter — November on the high tops can already see snow — that both male and female turn white. The only break in their white camouflage is their black tail.

The male has a black slash which runs from its gape through its eye. Both birds have bright red wattles. Truly a bird specialized for its environment, not only does the ptarmigan take on its amazing camouflage, but it also has feathered legs and feet. Like an Eskimo wearing sealskin boots, the feathers insulate the feet in the extreme cold and give them wonderful grip when walking on ice or snow. The ptarmigan makes a sound similar, but much less audible than the grouse, and it would best be described as a growling 'kuu-kuu-kuurrrrrr'.

Cock ptarmigan weigh from 550 to 650 g, the average weight being 600 g. Hen ptarmigan weigh from 500 to 620 g with an average weight of 580 g.

Like the grouse the ptarmigan has a tendency to stay within a fairly restricted range, living its life at two levels, the high tops in summer and lower levels during the winter. In summer on the high tops it feeds on the heathers and the restricted plants and berries that grow at that altitude. It also takes insects. Ptarmigan will readily fly to a lower level of the mountain if food there is more plentiful, but by mid-morning they would normally have moved back up to their normal range. In winter they move down to a lower level because of the depth of snow and harshness of winds and temperatures in their summer range.

Like the other game birds the ptarmigan has rounded wings, and when put up will fly with typical game bird flight of rapid wing beats interspersed with gliding periods on bowed wings. If put up ptarmigan will fly well forward along a ridge and out of sight. They are not easily walked up — they will either sit tight so that you walk right over them unless you have a particularly good dog, or they will jump and whizz off whilst still out of range.

I have shot ptarmigan, although only with the justification of collecting them for a museum. The sportsman must decide if the local population is sufficiently abundant to allow cropping.

The recommended cartridge size is 6 or 7.

To see ptarmigan in their
winter white the sportsman
must climb to the 'high tops'.

Ptarmigan.

Cock pheasant.

Pheasant (*Phasianus colchicus*)

There are many different pheasant species throughout the east, from China west through Turkey and the Caucasus. Some species are highly localized, while others are more widely spread. Some are relatively dull, others are extremely showy. Some are common, others rare. There is no other game bird that engenders such enthusiasm with breeders and collectors. Indeed it was due to these breeders and collectors that one species, having been driven almost to the point of extinction in its native Vietnam during the war with the United States, was saved. It was the collectors in the West who bred it for release back into its native land.

The pheasant which is familiar to the British, European and American field sportsman is the 'ring-neck pheasant' or one of the many variations of this particular species. The influences of the 'old English pheasant', which was originally the most popular in Britain, can be seen in the darker plumaged birds, though whether they have any link with the old English species is debatable, there being so many different colour variations to be seen throughout the country. Indeed, on looking through a number of birds shot on an estate on the same day to select one for the purposes of taxidermy, I picked out six birds all with different colour variations — yet all had come from the same source. Indeed, one local estate which gets its birds from a large pheasant breeder every year has a fair smattering of pheasants that are either melanistic or albino (black or white).

The cock bird is particularly colourful with an iridescent copper breast, bottle green head, bright red face patches and dark green rump before his long barred 45 cm tail. The hen has a shorter tail and is not brightly coloured, being brown, varying from dark chocolate mottle to light tan.

Most country dwellers are familiar with the pheasant's call. His noisiest time occurs when he is going up to roost in the evening, when he makes a considerable noise, calling or crowing, often followed by fairly noisy wing beating. Cocks call at dawn, particularly in spring, although their familiar sound of 'kok-kok-kok' can be heard throughout the year. One particular time when cock birds will make their 'kok-kok' followed by noisy rapid wing beating is in spring, when they are in the company of a hen.

The weight of a pheasant varies considerably, depending on age, food and location. An average cock bird weighs 1,200 g, although birds as heavy as 2,000 g or as light as 600 g may be found. Equally with hens size can vary from 700 g to 1,550 g although the average hen weighs around 1,000 g.

You will find pheasants in almost every part of Britain and Ireland. Indeed, the only areas where you will not find the bird is in the high mountains of Scotland, where the weather and environment are unsuitable. Since there are up to 15 million pheasants released annually in Britain, there is constant replenishment of wild stock, so it would be difficult to say how many wild birds there are throughout the country — as wild birds are shot annually their numbers are augmented by introduced birds.

The pheasant's natural preferrred habitat is lush grassy areas around river estuaries. The perfect example in Scotland is around the Endrick estuary where the mix of food, shelter and water is perfect. Another good area for the pheasant is the Fens. Indeed, if there is a marshy area about it seems always to hold a few birds. However, the pheasant has taken to our British countryside and

White pheasant with bit fitted to beak to prevent feather picking.

thrives where there is a mixture of open ground for food and thick woodland or shrubland where it can get shelter.

In the wild pheasants take a wide range of foods — plant seeds, leaves and fruit, new-sown corn and peas, beechmast, acorns, rowan berries, hips, nuts, most insects, caterpillars, worms, leatherjackets. Indeed, anything that is edible and catches the pheasant's eye is likely to be eaten.

Whether you are a rough shooter with a few pheasants on your ground, getting the thrill of your dog working them out of cover and the delight of taking two or three birds home for the pot, or whether you shoot them in large numbers at driven shoots, the pheasant provides quite wonderful sport to the shooting community throughout Britain, much of Europe and the United States.

My own personal taste varies between the delight of these two types of pheasant shooting. I love the thrill of a wild cock bird bursting from cover as I shoot on my own with my dog on a crisp November day. But equally, to stand at a peg on a driven shoot, where the birds are well presented, making testing and exciting shooting, is a great delight, although I believe that there is more to a pheasant shoot than just good birds, well presented. Much of what makes a driven day memorable are the other ingredients of the day — the company, the weather, other game seen, the location. Indeed the size of the bag has little to do with the day — better to have had a few exciting sporting birds than numerous less challenging shots.

The recommended cartridge size is 5 or 6.

A typical scene during a pheasant drive.

Grey partridge (*Perdix perdix*)

The grey partridge is a delightful little bird and for me rivals the pheasant as being synonymous with British game shooting traditions. Whilst it is widespread in parts of Britain, particularly England, up through central Scotland and the east coast, the partridge is not found in the highlands and islands. In Ireland the partridge can only be found in a few localized areas, as in Wales where there are some areas where the bird cannot be found at all.

Partridge numbers have greatly decreased from the late 1950s. During the 1960s, the era of the research chemist, many varieties of chemical fertilizers were delivered to the agricultural community and an emphasis on modernization and efficiency changed the face of farming. Hedgerows disappeared by the kilometre and the traditional areas that had been common on farms, the fallow areas and meadowland, were suddenly under pressure to yield crops, and so were ploughed, sprayed and taken into the overall farming strategy. Simultaneously, as farming changed, the

A particularly beautiful example of a European game cart. Feathered game is hung on one side and ground game on the other.

traditional farm with a bit of everything — cattle, sheep, arable — disappeared. Emphasis was put on specialization and many of the sheep disappeared from the low ground. The result was that the land was left open for the use of insecticides and fungicides. These chemicals dramatically increased yields, but reduced much of the insect life that had traditionally lived on the arable land. The insect food source dried up, and much that was left was impregnated with quantities of chemicals that were harmful to the partridge. The cumulative effects, including infertility, caused a dramatic reduction in numbers.

The partridge has not adapted so well to the changing habitat in Britain. In the traditional British farm, with its variety of crops and stock in small fields separated with hedgerows, the partridge flourished, since it needs a variety of food and cover. In areas where this sort of environment is still prevalent, partridge numbers are invariably high. It does not like the areas of England which have become almost prairie-like.

Whilst the decline of the partridge stocks of Britain have been described and are well documented, the blame being laid on the

Grey partridge.

use of chemicals and farm mechanization, the bottom line is that the bird's habitat has been dramatically altered. The partridge's food source has largely disappeared and its food is particularly critical. Seeds and grains of grasses and cereals are an important part of the partridge diet as are insects and grubs. In common with most birds, partridge eggs hatch at the same time as there is an abundance of the appropriate food source. The young partridge is so reliant on insect life that the eggs are timed to hatch in mid-June, when insect life is at its most abundant.

An enduring memory that most people have of the partridge is the sound of their typical call. Normally made at dusk, the 'kerrik, kerrik, kerrik' is familiar wherever partridge are found. However, partridge can make variations of this basic 'kerrik' when they are alarmed, as they rise or are in flight.

The typical picture people have of partridge is of a group of small round birds sitting or pecking about in a covey, or alternatively of one or two birds running away in alarm, heads erect, necks stretched in an upright fashion. Another typical image of the partridge is of a group of birds suddenly jumping from cover and whirring away, flying with their small round wings beating quickly, interspersed with gliding on set wings.

Grey partridge are seldom seen on their own; they are normally in a covey.

They are in fact happier running from danger and seem reluctant to fly, preferring to crouch motionless, relying on their immobility and camouflage to avoid detection, though ready to run off when appropriate. Often this running is preliminary to a sudden jump into the air and away they go.

The partridge is a plump little bird, although with its tendency to fluff out its feathers, it can have the appearance of a rounded fluffy ball. Weight variation with both cock and hen partridge is fairly small. Cock birds can weigh anything from 360 g to 430 g, a good average bird being 400 g. The hen birds' weight range would be from 320 g to 400 g, with an average hen weighing 375 g.

The partridge is basically a brown and grey bird. Both hen and cock are similar in plumage, the hen bird being slightly more subtle in coloration. Partridges can most typically be recognized by the clearly marked horseshoe on the breast, though hen birds sometimes do not have one. Their flanks are barred reddish brown on grey. Both birds have a reddish brown face, the cock bird having a grey-brown top on his head.

As a game bird the partridge is highly desirable. This is something of a contradiction in that although it is the slowest flying game bird, when driven it is arguably the most difficult to shoot. Being small, and with its ability to change direction suddenly, it is highly challenging and is to be valued as good sport.

Whilst shooting partridge is highly challenging, in Britain the wise sportsman would only consider shooting this bird if it were either reared and put down in number, or if the local population could stand gentle cropping. It should be said, however, that the caring sportsman would rather see these birds given every possible opportunity to regenerate than shoot them. However, there are vast numbers of grey partridge in northern Spain, and the serious shooter who wanted to experience these birds at their most numerous and challenging should go there.

The recommended shot size is 6 or 7.

Redlegged partridge (*Alectoris rufa*)

The redlegged or French partridge, sometimes known as the Guernsey, is a most attractive and colourful little bird which is now well established throughout southeast England. The redleg is also to be found on the east coast of England as far north as Darlington and as far west as Shrewsbury. In this area it has been highly successful and is now more numerous and well established in parts of eastern England than our own native grey partridge. Pockets of redlegs can be found in other areas, mainly in the eastern parts of England and Scotland as far north as Inverness, but these pockets are localized, the birds being the successful progeny of birds introduced by estates and shoot owners. The reason for the partridge's reluctance to spread west or do well there would appear to be the redleg's aversion to areas of high rainfall.

Contrary to what is popularly believed, the redleg is not a new arrival. It was first introduced in the late seventeenth century and by the eighteenth and nineteenth centuries introductions were relatively common. The redleg does not enjoy quite the affection of its grey cousin in the eyes of British sportsmen. There are various complaints made about it, notably that it is not such a good flier, and that it does not afford such good sport as the grey since it prefers to use its ability to run out of danger rather than to fly. It is this obvious reluctance to fly on the part of the redleg that marks it out from the grey. Greys whilst running can

English partridge with bit fitted to beak to prevent feather picking.

be made to fly quite easily. Redlegs conversely are often so reluctant to fly that on shoots where they are present, it is necessary to drive them. Indeed redlegs do not make good birds for walking up.

The bird is a native of parts of Europe and is found in France, Spain and northwestern Italy as well as the island of Corsica, although it is constantly being introduced to other areas as an adaptable game species.

The redleg is a more colourful bird than the grey, particularly with its white face patches, black eye stripe and most distinctive white, black and reddish brown flanks. It does not have the horseshoe mark on the breast. The legs and feet are a delightful salmon red as is the bill. The only discernible difference between the cock and hen birds is that the cock bird has a small spur. The redleg is indistinguishable from the grey at distance, as both its running movement and wing action are the same.

Slightly larger than the grey the redleg cock weighs 490–550 g, the average bird being 520 g. Hens weigh 380–480 g, the average hen weighing 440 g.

The call of the male is fairly distinctive, with a sound of 'chuck' repeated several times, or a 'kur, kur' sound, particularly when alarmed.

The redleg is attracted to much the same environment as the grey, but has a marked preference for a drier soil. The redleg's food is much less varied than the grey's, being mainly leaves and the seeds of both grasses and cereals, with less emphasis on insects, although they are eaten.

Admittedly there are aspects of the redleg which could be criticized in a comparison with the grey. I do feel it is wrong to compare the two birds. In its own right, in an area where there are no greys, it is a splendidly sporting little bird, with much to commend it and probably its lack of popularity in some areas stems from its other name, 'French partridge'. Brits do have a tendency to be reluctant to give credence or admire something 'foreign' over an indigenous species!

The recommended shot size for redleg partridge is 6 or 7.

Woodcock (*Scolopax rusticola*)

The woodcock is a delightful bird and there can be few field sportsmen who don't enjoy seeing it. Indeed the woodcock is so popular that whole books have been written about its habits and habitat.

There are woodcock from Japan, throughout the USSR and across Europe. Although not normally found around the Mediterranean coast, there are woodcock on the island of Corsica. They are found throughout Britain, although they tend to be more abundant in specific areas where the environment is more attractive to the species. Although common from the Lake District to the northern central highlands of Scotland, it does have a tendency to stay out of the higher regions during the harsher months. There are, strangely, one or two areas in Britain and Ireland where for some reason there are no woodcock. Cornwall and Devon have few birds and the southwestern tip of Ireland around the counties of Kerry and Cork have a restricted number of birds. The native population is augmented annually by the influx of substantial numbers from northern Europe.

The colour variation in woodcock is fairly extensive, ranging

This painting is entitled *Right and Left?*, referring to the unseen bird in the foreground flushed by the spaniel. Will the sportsman see it? Will he manage a right and left?

Woodcock are so well camouflaged and sit so tight on their nest you can easily walk past.

from a dark red brown with black barring to lighter browns and greys — it has on its plumage multiple shades of brown. The woodcock has one major contradiction in its physical appearance: although it is a wader and has the wader's typical long bill, it does not, however, have wader's long legs — it has short legs. A most striking physical attribute of the woodcock is its large bright black eyes. The positioning of the woodcock's eye gives it unusually good sight with a full 360 degree field of vision.

It usually has a strong bill about 70–75 mm long, although woodcock are reported every year with shorter bills. There seems to be nothing wrong with these birds — they appear to be nothing other than unusual variations of the norm.

Woodcock weights appear to have great variation. The cock's weight range is 265–356 g, with the average weight being 310 g. The hen bird's weight range is 275–425 g, with a good average hen weighing 330 g.

Woodcock have quite a distinctive rounded appearance. In flight they have broad wings and a short roundish body. Other than when being put up during a shoot, they are usually spotted flying when they are roding over tree tops, giving out distinctive croaking sounds which lead into a sharp 'tssiiwik'. This is repeated several times and can be heard over wide distances.

Roding takes place at dawn and, probably more commonly, at dusk from March to the end of June. Roding is not fully understood. It is most likely that the male bird is over-flying his area, calling to advertise his presence to a hen bird.

The woodcock's preference is for deciduous woodland and it is often found on bracken-covered areas particularly if spotted with deciduous trees. They also seem to have a preference for birch wood, oak and beech. The woodcock is normally found on dry ground with easy access to wet soft areas, where it can search with its highly adapted bill for earthworms which make up the bulk of its diet, although it will also take most insects and their larvae. The woodcock will also eat some vegetation, berries, grasses and seeds.

There is a question often raised about the woodcock: does it or does it not carry its young? No debate is necessary — it certainly does. Many people have witnessed this, including myself on several occasions separated by a period of years. Indeed, the first time I saw a woodcock carrying its young, I was too young to know anything about the so-called 'debate'. The most popular theory as to why it carries its young is that it is moving the chick out of danger or over an obstacle. I do not believe that to be the

Woodcock.

case. I think the explanation is much simpler, that the woodcock is simply sitting with a chick or chicks tucked under it for security. The adult bird suddenly jumps from cover and the chick is caught between the bird's legs. The adult bird then flies off. The weight and size of the chick and the security of the grip govern whether the chick drops after a few metres, whether the adult lands after a short distance, or whether the adult flies on carrying the chick. One such woodcock I witnessed carried its chick a good 40 metres out of my sight.

Most woodcock are probably shot during pheasant drives when the cry goes up 'woodcock!' and it certainly is a highly sporting bird. When flushed, woodcock rise very quickly and fly fast, normally in an erratic fashion, jerking in flight as they dash off through the trees. The woodcock is a particularly succulent bird on the table.

Worthy of note is the collectability of its pin feathers. It has a small tight feather that grows at the base of the first quill on each wing. This feather, known as a pin feather, is narrow, pointed and was at one time highly prized by artists, particularly those who painted miniatures. The finely tipped feather would be bound carefully into the end of a thin shaft, at the quill, giving the artist a finely balanced delicate little brush.

The recommended shot size for woodcock is 7.

The common snipe (*Gallinago gallinago*)

The tiny snipe is surely one of the most testing birds on the game list because of both its size and flight characteristics. It is found on the American continents from Argentina to northern Canada and Alaska. It is also found across northern Europe and as far east as Japan.

The common snipe is found throughout Britain. Typical snipe country is the flat boggy moorland and mosses of northern Scotland and the west of Ireland. At one time the snipe was much more numerous throughout the country, until the changing and modernizing of farming methods and the draining of the myriad wet areas had a devastating effect on so much of our wildlife. At one time much of the arable land in Britain was lined with many little streams, and this water was used to top up the drinking ponds that were necessary for agricultural animals. After the widespread use of irrigation and piping and the introduction of ball-cock controlled troughs much of the natural wet areas disappeared. This had an obvious detrimental effect on the snipe population and in the more highly productive areas, particularly the south of England, the bird began to disappear.

Another threat to the best habitats of the snipe in Ireland is the growth in the peat cutting industry. Vast areas of bogland have been disrupted as the peat is cut, dried and bagged, either as a commercial fuel or to be exported as a gardening additive. In Scotland, particularly in the northern Flow Country, one of the penalties paid for the widespread drainage and afforestation has been considerable loss of boggy habitat which has had a direct effect on snipe numbers.

The snipe has, however, re-established itself in the south, although it is not as numerous there as in areas from the

Snipe.

Midlands north through the Lake District and into central Scotland, where it is so common that there are few wet areas that do not hold a snipe or two.

Like the woodcock the snipe has striking large black eyes, giving it all-round vision. Probably the most notable feature of the plumage of the snipe is its striped head. Both male and female have similar plumage, a mixture of brown and buff in stripes with bars, and a distinctive cream coloured double V on their back. It has a very long bill, $2\frac{1}{2}$ times the length of its head. It is in its distinctive fast zig-zag flight that you would normally see the white of its outer tail feathers.

Tiny birds, both male and female are similar in weight and size. Their weight range is 95–125 g, the average weight being about 118 g.

Snipe do not make much noise, although when flushed they can give a fairly loud 'skaap, skaap'. During spring they are more vocal and will give out repeated 'chuper, chuper' sounds. Another sound which is often assumed to be made by the snipe's voice but which has nothing to do with anything vocal, is the vibrating or humming noise heard as the bird dashes through the air, normally on its downward flight at a steep angle. The sound is produced by the air rushing over the outer tail feathers and is often known as 'drumming'. You can hear this sound throughout the year but it is more common during the breeding season.

The snipe has a sophisticated bill and takes a wide variety of foods, the bulk of which is worms, but water beetles and moist ground insects of a wide variety are eaten as are small molluscs, berries and seeds.

With its high-speed zig-zag flight the snipe is a particularly testing target. However, for me it is one of those birds that, if I was in any doubt as to its numbers locally, I would tend not to shoot. Conversely, if I were in an area where the bird is known to be numerous and the population capable of withstanding cropping, then I would certainly enjoy the sport.

The recommended shot size for snipe is 8. (It would be unlikely, unless you were going shooting snipe specifically, that you would have shot of the recommended size. You would be more likely to encounter snipe when shooting duck and therefore would be more likely to be loaded with a shot size considerably heavier.)

Golden plover (*Pluvialis apricaria*)

Of the three waders on the British game list, golden plover, snipe and woodcock, the golden plover is the one which is seen and probably shot least by sportsmen, due to the area in which it lives. Found primarily in northern Europe, from Russia through Scandinavia, Britain and Iceland, the bird winters in the warmer areas of western Europe, some birds migrating as far south as North Africa.

In Britain, although found in a few parts of Wales, Exmoor, the

Lake District and western Ireland, it is really only found in strength in northern Scotland.

It is a pretty little bird with a short bill set on a large round head. The sexes are alike. In summer plumage they have a marked black face with black on the underparts. The upper part of the bird is distinctive and colourful, with gold and black speckles. When moulting into winter plumage, the black disappears and is replaced with underparts of white.

The golden plover is a vocal little bird. Its call is reminiscent of a lament, being variations of 'wee-wee' or 'kee-wee'.

In summer the birds are to be found on the grass areas of moorland, although I have also seen golden plover fairly high up in the Grampians at this time. In the winter they prefer to congregate in lowland fields and around our coasts and estuaries. Golden plover often join up and feed with lapwings, although if put up the two species quickly separate.

Golden plover take a wide variety of worms, insects, small molluscs and insect larvae, and a variety of grass and weed seeds and berries.

In the right situation, golden plover can be sporting birds. Their flight can be fairly erratic and typical of their kind, varying from fairly slow winging to sudden dropping, almost to ground level. They are normally shot when the gun is flighting coastal wildfowl or at evening or dawn flight inland.

The recommended shot size for golden plover is 7.

Woodpigeon (*Columba palumbus*)

There are three species of pigeon which may be shot in Britain, the feral pigeon, the collared dove and the woodpigeon. I do not intend to cover either the collared dove or feral pigeon, but to concentrate on the woodie, also called by its older name, the ring dove, a reference to its broken dog-collar of white feathers.

The woodpigeon is the cheapest and one of the most sporting birds the sportsman will find anywhere. Whether they are shot flighting into fields or when going into roost in a woodland, the woodpigeon can be highly sporting and enjoyable. The pigeon is in some areas a most serious pest to agricultural interests, accounting for enormous crop damage and cost per annum.

The bird is found across Europe from Scandinavia to the Urals and as far south as North Africa. It is found throughout Britain,

Woodpigeon over stubble.

with the exception of the outer islands of Scotland and the hill and mountain regions. Although found in Ireland, it is not quite as numerous.

Unlike many species that have paid the price for man's ever more successful and ruthless policy of getting the maximum production from his agricultural industry, the pigeon has been very much a success story, keeping pace with the changing face of agriculture. Indeed the reason for the growth in the pigeon population in Britain over the last century – which has gathered pace in the last 40 years – has been the changing and increasing agricultural picture of Britain. Vast areas of cereals and increasing growth of brassicas and root vegetables have all supplied the pigeon with an abundant food source and its population has risen accordingly.

Few people in Britain who have ventured out of the cities in the summer will not have heard the familiar 'coo-coo' of the woodie. It is a soft sound, which can be heard over wide distances. At first glance the pigeon appears to be uniformly grey, with the exception of the white feathering on each side of the neck. In flight it is easily identified with its white wing bar. The bird has a black tip on its tail with a paler underside, and the breast sometimes has a pinkish bloom on the feathering. The head and neck is bluer than the rest of the bird. Both sexes are similar.

Pigeons can have a wide weight range, depending on time of year and food availability. Male birds are normally within 470–650 g, with an average weight of 570 g. Female birds weigh 460–620 g with an average weight of 550 g.

The pigeon has the most remarkable hearing and eyesight. It is a bird well blessed with acute senses to detect predators since the bird's only method of defence is flight, which it does with great speed and ability. It is these senses, particularly of sight, that make it necessary for the pigeon shooter to be careful in the construction of a hide if he is to successfully shoot them over decoys.

Although originally a bird which was more dependent on deciduous woodland, the woodie has adapted in the most remarkable fashion to inhabit our agricultural areas. Wherever its favour diet, which is extensive, can be found, the pigeon will gravitate in that direction. As food availability rotates in the early spring the birds will go for a variety of foods from holly berries and winter corn to greens and clover, having a particularly delight for kale, sprouts, cabbages and other greens. As the year progresses and sowing takes place, the pigeon will eat turnip, rape, peas, beans, corn and mustard. Flattened grain fields and the patches which have been beaten down by harsh weather, called 'laid', are favourite areas for the pigeons to take grain. In other words, the pigeon has a most versatile appetite, with an enormous crop capacity in which to pack away large amounts of food. Surprising as it might seem, a pigeon can carry 60 acorns of mixed sizes in its crop. If you wish to see one of the reasons for the farmers' fury, shoot a bird flying off clover with a full crop, carefully open the crop and you will be surprised at the huge pile of greens.

Shooting pigeons is truly delightful sport and I can think of few more enjoyable experiences than sitting in warm weather in a hide in an autumn grain field, with a good flight of birds. They are cheap highly sporting birds, easy to pluck and succulent on the table. They also provide the serious pigeon shooter with an additional advantage: if he shoots a large number of birds, those in excess of his needs can be sold to a game dealer to recoup some of his cartridge costs.

The recommended shot size for woodpigeon is 6.

CHAPTER SEVEN

Wildfowl and Wildfowling

Purists would say that only coastal fowling is true wildfowling, and that inland shooting is not quite the same thing. It is certainly true that those hardy individuals who enjoy coastal fowling do put up with harsher conditions with less chance of shooting and certainly less chance of getting several birds.

Geese present a constant problem for the shooter who does not spend a great deal of time in close proximity to them — how to judge their size and range. Because they are so much larger than other wildfowl, the most common mistake made by even the most experienced shot is to assume that the birds are closer and travelling much more slowly than they are. This is an illusion which has fooled goose shooters since men first tried to shoot them on the wing.

FORESHORE SHOOTING

Few foreshore shooters take the proper precautions before entering what is a dangerous environment, confusing discomfort and lack of preparation with the image of the sport. Few coastal fowlers would consider carrying a compass and pocket flare, or checking tide tables and weather with the coastguard, or any of the other commonsense safety details. Annually a few field sportsmen lose their lives. Many more get into difficulties, sometimes causing the emergency services to become involved, occasioning unnecessary, costly and time-consuming rescue operations that could have been avoided.

The most benign shore which you may have visited in summer can take on a totally different complexion in winter. On one occasion when I was out on some mudflats a mist blew in, enveloping myself and my companion in a grey formless world. My companion was quite adamant as to the direction we should take to shore: my compass showed that he would have been walking parallel with the shoreline.

If you are considering a coastal fowling expedition it is wise to run over a simple checklist.

1   Inform someone of where you are going to be and of your expected arrival time back.

2   Check the tides with the coastguard.

3   Carry a small pocket flare, available from any good sport or diving shop.

4   If you are going to be in a boat you MUST wear a lifejacket.

5   Carry a compass and know how to use it.

6   If shooting in the company of others, first locate the nearest WORKING telephone. If your companion gets into difficulties and you rush off looking for a telephone, valuable time can be lost. More importantly, having arrived at the telephone box is not the time to discover it is not working.

Water conducts heat 25 times faster than air. If you think how cold you can get standing about on a winter's day for 25 minutes, it would only take one minute for your body to reach the same temperature in water, that is assuming that the water temperature was the same as the air temperature. If the water is colder you have less time.

When shooting on the foreshore you will either be on the dunes or sea wall above the tidal mark, out on the flats of the tidal area when the tide is low, or in a boat. It is wise to have a look at where you intend to shoot the day before. Observe whether the birds favour an area for flying over. In the morning flight birds fly out to feeding grounds and the direction they take depends on the wind and their intended destination. Take note of the direction the majority of birds come from, the time, wind direction and general conditions. After the flight is over, make your way to the area you have observed most birds passing over and decide where best to build your hide the following morning.

If you are going to shoot from the tidal area it is wise, prior to an early morning arrival laden with equipment, to try and check the consistency of the sand or mud, to see if it is passable, and to work out where you will position yourself.

The following morning arrive pre-dawn and get in position. As the light starts to strengthen, do not be tempted to start moving around looking for a better position. You have committed yourself. To start looking for a better site is pointless and you run the risk of alerting the birds to your presence. Irrespective of what movement there is or how good the flight might be, keep your eye on both the tide and time. Do not be tempted to give yourself an extra ten minutes. The walk back, when you are cold and have been sitting for a while, always seems to take longer. If you are unfortunate enough to be caught in a mist or fog on the foreshore, stop shooting, check your compass bearings and go to the beach.

If you are going to use a boat it is ill-advised to use a small dinghy. If you are with a companion the more experienced of you should act as boat handler. Make sure you wear your lifejacket – accidents seldom give you enough time to start looking under the seat for it. If you are using an outboard engine (having checked engines are permissible locally), ensure the boat is equipped with both oars and rowlocks and do not overload the boat. It is ill-advised to take a dog in a boat. It is of no practical use and just gets in the way. Ensure the boat has an anchor.

In addition to any small pocket flare that you may have, ensure that the boat is also equipped with a flare.

INLAND GOOSE SHOOTING

Geese roost on water at night, flying out in the mornings to the fields they are currently feeding on. They spend the day feeding, before returning at night to their roost. Therefore there are really only two points in the day when the wildfowler has any serious chance of intercepting them – dawn or dusk.

If you intend to shoot geese over decoys (morning flighting) it is first necessary to spy the land where they are feeding, looking for the direction from which they come and what areas they actually land on first since it is essential to try to get the birds as they come in, not after they have landed and then begin to move on. Take the prevailing wind direction into account. Geese prefer landing into the wind: a goose landing into the wind has greater manoeuvrability either to make a smooth landing, or to aid a speedy departure.

Look for any natural cover to give you a background – low bushes, hedgerows, ditches – anywhere that can be used as a backdrop. Avoid tall trees – not only do they give you an area through which you cannot shoot, but generally geese will not come in and land with tall trees in front of them. Select the spot where you want to build your hide and, if you are unfamiliar with the area, try to make a mental note of any geographical features – straining posts, gaps in hedges, gates – since it is essential that you set up before dawn. There is nothing more annoying than, having planned the exercise beforehand, erected your hide under cover of darkness and set out your decoys, to discover, as the light strengthens, that you did not take note of the landmarks carefully enough and you have put yourself 100 metres or so to one side of where you observed the passing geese on the previous day!

There are many proprietary hides on the market and whether you buy one or make it yourself, the construction is the same. You will require four good footrods plus a decent length of light camouflage netting. It is always preferable to position your hide in front of a backdrop, so that you are sitting against it and can watch what is in front of you without moving. If on the other hand you are BEHIND an obstacle such as a wall or bush, you must bob your head about to see what is coming and movement such as this must be avoided. With all shooting and stalking the rule applies that if you can see your quarry, your quarry can see you, except of course if you are sitting motionless peering through a spy hole in a camouflage net. Therefore, always position yourself in front of cover. Put your footrods firmly into the ground as close to your background as is sensibly possible approximately 1.5 metres apart. Carefully hang your net on the uprights. Keep it taut so that it does not flap in the wind and anchor it with tent pegs or stones.

The size of your hide is personal preference. I prefer a hide to have plenty of room with a small area for my dog to sit in, my seat and sufficient ground space where I can lay out my gear – cartridge bag, game bag, flask, cup. Obviously a hide should be as small and inconspicuous as possible, but at the same time a compromise must be reached for comfort and manoeuvrability.

When you have built your hide try to make it blend as well as possible into the background. If you are against a hedgerow you may find it does not need any adornments. If on the other hand you are against a fence with long grass around it, then it is as well to thread some grass into the net, to keep it as invisible as possible. If you were shooting in snow it is better to wear white overalls and use a white sheet as a hide, or even better to create a snow wall by making large snowballs and sitting them one on top of the other, the balls getting smaller as they near the top of the wall.

Once you have put up your hide set out your decoy pattern. It is important to anyone who is going to use decoys to lure birds down into a field that they understand how a decoy layout works. The sight of decoys alone does not automatically ensure that passing birds will change direction and land beside you.

Decoys only work at specific times, normally when the birds are hungry or are looking for a place to land. If a skein of geese is travelling from point A, their roost, to point B, an intended feeding ground, they can fly over any number of decoys and, apart from the odd curious call, give no indication that they have noticed them. Conversely, if the birds are actually looking for a place to feed, then decoys can add that extra convincing attraction to make them land in one field in preference to any other. Being gregarious, if they wish to land, they will be more likely to join other birds already on the ground. Therefore before you intend to pursue the birds a study of the ground beforehand, preferably the day before, is important.

You will often notice that birds show a preference for one side of a field as opposed to another. Sometimes the reasons are fairly obvious in that geese prefer not to come in and land beside tall trees. Sometimes the reason is impossible to fathom and one can only assume it has to do with minerals in the soil.

You may also discover, through observation, that geese repeatedly land in one part of a field then walk to another before settling and starting to feed. All these peculiarities you must take into account before deciding where you are going to set up your hide.

Pay attention to the wind. Geese greatly prefer landing into the wind since their streamlined bodies are designed to cut into a head wind. A tail wind for instance means they have to work a great deal harder to stay in the air.

Many people theorize about the correct pattern in which

decoys should be laid out, but the real answer is that there is no magic formula. The only guidelines you must keep in mind when laying out decoys is that the pattern should be irregular when viewed from above. Birds coming in to join your decoys are going to recognize something is amiss if you have set out a perfect circle, for instance, so lay the decoys in an irregular pattern, either in an elongated oval or in a rough fan shape.

Some decoys are realistic, with lovely feathered texture finishes. This means nothing to the goose and is purely to catch the eye and the pocket of the buyer. In the United States it is not uncommon for wildfowlers in some states to lure snowgeese by pegging out sheets of newspaper, the white dots being sufficient to bring the birds down. Most sportsmen are aware that milk bottles painted matt grey and laid in a pea field is all that is needed to bring pigeons whizzing in. It is the pattern you create in your decoy set-up which is important.

When setting out decoys it is advisable to place the layout slightly past the hide into the wind. Most geese coming in to join a party on the ground come in to the rear of the birds already down and by putting the decoy set-up to one side you draw the birds down and past the front of your hide, within range.

Experience will teach you know to read a particular combination of topography and wind which may dictate the distance the decoys should be from your hide. A good instance of this is on my own ground. With a strong easterly wind the only cover is under a hedge, directly under the path that approaching geese will take.

It is therefore necessary in this situation to place the decoy set-up well out in the field, a good 90 metres behind my hide, so that the approaching birds can see them clearly while still a distance off. Yet at first glance to see me put my decoys so far away you could be forgiven for thinking I did not know what I was doing. However, with this set-up I have enjoyed some of the most electrifying flighting.

As a general rule for range keep your decoys within 30 metres, having the furthest birds at a paced distance to aid with judging range when the birds start to flight in. Remember the idea with decoys is to draw the birds slightly past your hide so that you are drawing them as close as possible.

Having set out your decoys make sure your hide is comfortable and neat. Set your loaded gun carefully to one side, making sure that you put it in a position where it cannot be knocked over. Remember that shooting geese from a hide is the only occasion when it is permissible to lay down a loaded gun.

If you are going to use a call there is little point in giving your own version of the dawn chorus. Calls are not, contrary to some people's belief, a magical way of producing birds. They are only an aid to drawing passing birds' attention to your decoys. If birds are passing a few honks may help draw their attention to the decoys. If they show no interest do not blow continuously; it will have no effect. Geese will only join decoys in a field out of hunger. If they are looking for a place to land you may entice them down beside you. If they are not feeding in your area, or are speeding on their way to parts unknown, you will not bring them down no matter how hard you try.

Conversely, if geese are hungry or decide for some reason that your field is irresistible, a few toots can have a quite astonishing and magical effect. I have turned skeins hundreds strong on a few toots, and so keen were they to come down, that rather than glide or circle, lowering themselves at a leisurely pace, they have wiffled right down on top of me. (Wiffling is the term used when geese want to go straight down at speed. Aiming themselves towards the ground, they spill the air from their wings, dropping at high speed, as they zig-zag towards the earth, at the last minute catching themselves and dropping their paddles before landing.)

When geese start to glide in towards decoys I have seen even the strongest men turn to jelly. The secret of mastering this particular moment is to be cool. Pick up your gun and watch the birds approach through the net (as described in Chapter 1 under Shooting Technique).

Morning flight can last from a few minutes of busy activity to an apparent limitless time, as stream after stream of birds keep coming in for most of the morning. The reasons for this are either that there is insufficient food where the birds have been feeding, compelling them to search for more, or that they are being disturbed and have moved on. Normally one would expect the morning flight to be pretty well over by around 9 a.m.

Birds hungry for food are more likely to be easily brought in to decoys, and this is where the shooter must practise self-discipline and restraint. It is wrong to shoot all morning, justifying the exercise by your lack of success on previous outings. The true fowler is as interested in conservation and the future of the birds as he is in having good sport, and two birds per flight should be regarded as plenty.

The weather affects the type of food that geese are likely to

take. When they first arrive the bulk of birds show a marked preference for barley stubbles, and as they clean the grain from the stubble and the stubbles are ploughed in they will move to grass and winter wheat. In areas where carrots, turnips and potatoes are grown, they will eat them, particularly once they have been softened by frost. Pinkfoot have a preference for grain, grass and potatoes, and only when they are really pressed by severe hunger have I seen them eating other foods.

Due to their size, geese can give the sportsman the false impression of being closer and moving more slowly than they are. These geese are greylag.

GEESE

The greylag goose (*Anser anser*)

The greylag goose is for most wildfowlers the king of the grey geese. Whether they pursue these large elegant grey birds on the foreshore or over decoys on inland fields, the greylag goose offers the excitement and spectacle all goose shooters look for.

The greylag is the only native British goose that breeds here. Today the breeding grounds of the British greylag are severely restricted to the more remote parts of northwest Scotland − in the Outer Hebrides, Sutherland, Caithness and Ross & Cromarty, the largest concentrations being at Loch Druidibeg, South Uist.

The birds are undoubtedly the remnants of the much larger breeding flocks which colonized the entire country hundreds of years go, including Ireland, but, mainly because of land reclamation and over-shooting, the birds have gradually moved north to some of the most inaccessible parts of Scotland. The native birds do not appear to migrate but remain around their breeding ground throughout the year.

The breeding range of the greylag goose is generally further south than other geese, in Iceland, Scandinavia, Eastern Europe and Russia. These birds mostly winter to the south of their breeding grounds, and the bulk of the British winter migrants are from Iceland, although a small number occasionally migrate to the east coast of England from Scandinavia and Eastern Europe. As with the pinkfoot, Britain is extremely fortunate in having the *entire* Icelandic population of greylags wintering here.

The bulk of migrant greylags are found in Scotland, especially when they first arrive in September to November. Some birds spend a short time in Scotland before moving south to the north of England or west to Ireland. The birds return to their breeding grounds in April and like the pinkfoot seem to have established flight lines for their journey home.

The greylag could be confused with the whitefront at a distance, since both species look similar and both can have a considerable colour variation amongst their own kind. A pale-headed Greenland whitefront (which has a less distinct white face marking) could easily be confused with a greylag. Distinction between the two is made even more difficult for it is not uncommon to find a few Greenland whitefronts amongst a flock of greylags or pinkfoot.

The overall impression of the greylag is of a greyish brown bird with a neck and head that is a soft light grey. The neck has the diagonal lines caused by feather indentations. The back of the bird is grey brown with a barring effect caused by the pale edgings of the wing coverts. The underbelly of the greylag is a lighter grey white with black blotches, which can sometimes be heavy enough to describe them as bars, although they are rarely as noticeable or pronounced as on the whitefront. The tail coverts, both upper and lower, are white, which contrast quite markedly with the dark grey tail feathers. The bill of the bird is deep and heavy, almost triangular in shape and pale orange in colour. The legs and feet of the greylag are pink, and the eyes are brown with a distinct orange circle around the eye socket.

The male and female are of similar colour, although the male is

A good winter morning's bag, 4 brace of greylag, 2½ brace of cock pheasants.

generally larger, and weighs around 2,500–4,000 g with an average weight of 3,500 g. The female greylag weighs around 2,000–3,800 g with an average weight of 3,000 g.

The greylag is probably the species of grey goose about which there is more nonsense spoken than any other. It is said that they are highly intelligent birds, and that there is always a leader in the flock, usually an old gander. This is not the case. Greylags, like other geese, form distinct family groups within a flock, but there is no 'flock leader'. Nor do they post guards to watch over the flock as it feeds. As with other wild grazing animals, a few birds will always have their heads up whilst others are eating.

The greylag are the least likely of the grey geese to remain in the distinct V formation as they tend to prefer to fly in a diagonal line.

The greylag follows the same feeding pattern as the pinkfoot and is dependent on modern agriculture for its survival. They start on stubble, move on to grass and then eat the potatoes left in the field, particularly those that are frosted. In Scotland they can sometimes be observed competing with the sheep as they feed on the swede turnips. I have seen these geese so intent on this feeding that they ignore the farmer as he comes to tend his sheep. Their strong broad bill makes eating these hard tubers a relatively easy task.

The greylag is a daytime feeder, flighting in from its roost at first light and returning at dusk. When the moon is full they can reverse this procedure and feed at night by the light of the moon, returning to their roost at dawn.

The flight of the greylag, though swift and direct, is generally more heavy in appearance than other geese. However this does not detract from their aerial abilities, as these birds can take off and land as swiftly as any other goose.

When the grey geese are on a high migration flight it is difficult to distinguish pinkfoot from greylags, except for their call which one can hear as they fly high in the sky. The greylag goose has the most raucous call of all the grey geese and in flight the birds are quite vocal. The voice has a distinct similarity to the farmyard goose which is descended from the greylag. The call is a 'aahng-aahng-aahng', each syllable at a different pitch. The alarm call of the greylag is a single-pitched typical farmyard 'honk'. When feeding they also produce a conversational gobble sound.

A mated pair show great affection and remain together for life.

The greylag has the largest population of all the geese wintering in Britain, the average yearly numbers being just short of 100,000 and increasing.

The recommended shot size for this goose is 1 or 3.

Greylags in grass. Note the old car in the background right. This practice of leaving a vehicle in the field is to discourage geese from crops.

Pinkfooted geese in December sky.

Pinkfooted goose (*Anser brachyrhynchus*)

Although the areas where the pinkfoot is found are limited, the bird's highly gregarious nature means that pinkfoot concentrations can be very dense. The pinkfooted goose is often treated as a subspecies of the bean goose, as there is little to differentiate between the two. Even now leading ornithologists have not decided whether they are simply races of the same species or are two entirely separate species.

The range and distribution of the pinkfoot is limited, its breeding grounds being confined to Greenland, Iceland and Spitzbergen. The Spitzbergen birds migrate to winter in Denmark, West Germany and the Netherlands. Britain, however, has the *entire* Icelandic and Greenland population wintering here and most of these birds are found in Scotland.

The pinkfoot begins to arrive in Scotland in mid-September, through to November. There is considerable movement within the population on arrival here. The birds favour inland habitats initially before they move towards the coasts, and as winter progresses they tend to move south into England. Their movement is dependent on various factors, including the weather and the availability of food. The largest numbers of pinkfoot in the British Isles are found in the Perth and Kinross area of Central Scotland, the most important roost being a small loch just outside Perth, Dupplin Loch, where a staggering 25,500 geese have been counted. Other important roosts are at Strathbeg Loch and Meikle Loch at Newburgh, Carsebreck, north of Dunblance and Loch Leven, where many species of wildfowl, rare and common, are found in the winter.

Since the early 1970s an increasing number of pinkfoot have been travelling to Lancashire, where they have discovered that the carrot crop can provide them with an excellent source of food. The numbers travelling south have increased year after year, until they are now a pest to the carrot farmers there.

About 10,000 birds are found in the Solway Firth area, where the numbers are only now beginning to build again, after many pinkfoot moved elsewhere. Areas in England, which at one time supported large numbers, have more or less now been deserted by the birds, who have returned to Scotland, although small numbers can still be found in the Wash and the Humber estuary.

The type of habitat preferred by the pinkfoot is largely dependent on two things: availability of water to provide a safe roost and good arable ground to provide an adequate food supply. The birds roost either on estuaries, flighting in to arable ground from the coasts, or on inland waterways with good farming land nearby.

The pinkfoot is the smallest of the grey geese found in Britain, with only a minor size variation between the male and female. The male weighs from 1,800–3,300 g, with an average goose weighing 2,700 g. The female weighs between 1,750 and 3,200 g, with a good average being 2,250 g.

Both sexes are alike in colour. They have small heads and slender necks which are dark brown, much darker than the greylag. The breast is pinkish brown, merging with the darker back and pale grey/white belly. The overall impression of the pinkfoot is of a neat little goose with a light grey body and dark head and neck. It is the greyest of the grey geese and is the only *Anser* goose with a pink bill and pink legs, hence the name. It has a shorter bill than the other *Anser* species which may help to explain its more fastidious diet, unable as it is to probe with the strength of the bigger billed birds.

The staple diet of the pinkfoot is grass, seeds, roots and berries. It has a preference for grains, particularly barley, and has become increasingly dependent on the agricultural cycle for its food. As

the winter progresses the foods taken by the pinkfoot changes. Once the stubbles are ploughed in (later in Scotland than in England) the bird will turn to grass and potatoes — in this instance they can be a boon to the farmer as they clean up the fields of rotten and frosted potatoes.

In flight pinkfoot fly in the familiar V formation, often in large flocks, and can be recognized by their dark heads and pale bodies. They are noisy birds with a distinctive 'wink-wink' or 'pink-pink' call. When feeding the birds produce a quiet conversational buzzing sound.

To a great extent the pinkfooted goose has given up its natural feeding on marshlands, fresh and salt, and is now dependent on the whims of modern agriculture. However, having adapted its diet and habitat to suit this food source, there is no reason to suppose that it could not change again, if farmers decided to grow different crops. Like other geese, pinkfoot feed during the day, flighting in to their feeding grounds at dawn and returning to the roost at dusk, although during a full moon one can often see them grazing at night, when they will return to their roost at dawn.

The population of pinkfoot is healthy and the future of the bird looks good. The most recent bird surveys indicate that the numbers currently wintering in Britain top 100,000 and the birds are unlikely to suffer undue harm from the wildfowler.

The recommended shot size for this goose is 1 or 3.

Pinkfooted geese in Perthshire.

Whitefronted goose (*Anser albifrons*)

The whitefronts which winter in this country are divided into two sub-species – the Greenland whitefront and the European or Siberian whitefront. The lesser whitefront, another sub-species is worth a mention, for a few stragglers appear in this country with the whitefront flock, and are found mostly at Slimbridge in Gloucestershire.

The European whitefront is widely shot in the USSR and Europe where population numbers remain stable. The Greenland whitefront, on the other hand, appears to be declining in numbers due to poor breeding success.

The European whitefronts which arrive in Britain do so from early October to as late as January. They congregate in the south of England and South Wales.

The Greenland whitefront breeds in western Greenland, migrating to the UK in late autumn to winter along the west coasts of Scotland and Ireland. The most important wintering site for the Greenland whitefront is the Wexford Slobs, an area of reclaimed farmland, part of which the Irish government set up as a refuge for the geese. Islay, part of the Inner Hebrides, holds another important site for these geese, with others wintering in nearby Mull of Kintyre and in Galloway. Few Greenland whitefronts venture as far south as England.

Of all the species of goose wintering here, the whitefront causes the least damage to crops and other farmland. It is less partial to agricultural land, but prefers to winter near the coasts, in salt marshes and freshwater marshland, where it can do little damage.

Whitefront males are slightly larger than the females, the male weighing 1,700–3,300 g, averaging 2,500 g. The female weighs from 1,700–3,100 g, averaging 2,400 g.

Sexes are alike in colour, and are an overall grey brown, with black blotches and bars on the lower breast and belly. Some are so heavily barred they can appear to be completely black on the underparts. The whitefront adult bird has a distinctive white feathering around the bill, reaching up to the forehead. Both the upper and undertail coverts are white, with the tail feathers themselves of a dark brown colour, tipped with white. The legs and feet are orange, the bill is pink and the eyes dark brown.

Identification in flight is aided by the white forehead and black belly bars which can easily be recognized. Although they do resemble the greylag, the whitefront can be distinguished from the greylag by its overall darker colouring, its pink bill (the greylag's bill is orange) and its white face markings. The head of the whitefront is also smaller than the greylag's.

The Greenland has a slight colour variation: it is darker, more olive brown and has less distinct feathering on the face. The bill of the Greenland is more orange or orange-yellow. This makes the Greenland whitefront slightly more difficult to distinguish from the greylag.

The call of the whitefront is shriller than that of other geese. They have a high-pitched 'kow-yow' or 'kow-lyow' and are sometimes known as the laughing goose. When feeding the whitefront makes a great deal of noise, producing a kind of buzzing sound, the result of aggressive encounters when family groups meet, which is a good means of identification.

Like other geese the whitefront mates for life.

The European whitefront has had several good breeding seasons and appears to be on the increase, with a world population estimated to be anywhere between 750,000 and one million strong. The average winter population in Britain is from 4,000 to 8,000.

The Greenland on the other hand has suffered several poor breeding seasons, and is suffering a population decline. It is estimated that the total British winter population of Greenlands is around 8,000 with a further 7,000 wintering in Ireland. Of that 7,000 nearly 6,000 geese are concentrated in the Wexford Slobs.

The recommended shot size for this goose is 1 or 3.

Canada goose (*Branta canadensis*)

The Canada goose is the only *Branta* species that may be legally taken within a specified open season. The other two *Branta* geese, the barnacle and the Brent, can only be taken under special licence in areas where crop damage occurs.

The Canada, as its name suggests, is a native of North America, which was introduced to this country as early as the late seventeenth century, its handsome appearance making it popular with country landowners as ornamentation for their lakes and ponds.

It was obviously an adaptable bird for within 100 years of its introduction it had started to breed and multiply, and within another century there were many cases of pockets of feral geese breeding in England. Today they are well established over most of England, with smaller numbers in Scotland and Wales. Canadas do not move by their own volition to new grounds, preferring to stay where they are even in an overcrowded situation, so it is probable that man helped the colonization of the country by moving pairs of Canadas to new areas.

Of all the geese in this country the Canada is the species about which most complaints are made concerning crop damage. Whereas the greylag goose can do considerable damage to a field, it is only here over the winter months. The Canada goose on the other hand is a resident bird.

The Canada goose can be found throughout North America. It has the largest population of all the geese and its numbers have increased considerably since the 1950s. An intensive study of the Canada has been carried out to obtain a better understanding of the bird in order to manage the population more efficiently, and to provide sport for the wildfowler without damaging the overall numbers. The North American Canadas are all migratory, wintering directly to the south of their breeding grounds. The British population, however, is static.

The Canada goose is found in large concentrations in many parts of England, the largest flocks being in the lower Thames Valley, the Midlands, north Shropshire, Cheshire and Yorkshire, with little movement between flocks.

The most easily identifiable physical aspect of the Canada goose is the white chin strap which reaches from above the eye and right around the chin to the other side. The presence of the chin strap is the most obvious way to differentiate the Canada from the barnacle goose, which is of roughly the same colour. The Canada is the only goose with black on its head and neck. The barnacle has a completely white face, the white running across the eyes and right down to the bill, with only the top of its head remaining black.

The head and neck of the Canada are black, and the body brown. The legs and bill are black, and the bill is usually large and long, although it remains slender at the base, being designed for stripping and probing. The neck is long and slender, almost swan-like, running down to a lighter chest, although there can be considerable shade variation in the chest. The upper parts are a greyish brown, running down to a black tail, with the tail coverts, both upper and lower, being white.

The Canada is the largest of all the geese in this country. The female is slightly smaller than the male although they have the same colour of plumage. In flight the birds' large size and slow wing beat identify them as Canadas, although do not confuse the slow wing beat with slow movement, as the bird's flight is faster than it looks. The wings of the Canada are long and broad, and the long slender neck, when seen in flight, is characteristic of the bird.

The gander weighs from 4,000–5,550 g with an average weight of 4,750 g. The female weighs between 3,500 and 5,000 g, averaging 4,400 g. The juvenile Canada is of a duller appearance – even the chin strap is a dirty grey colour. Its plumage becomes adult in the first winter.

Like all other species of geese the Canada mates for life and does not become sexually mature until its second year. If one goose is killed before his or her mate, the other will almost certainly take another mate, sometimes within days or even hours of the loss.

Canada geese are highly gregarious sociable birds, and it is not uncommon to see flocks numbering several hundred feeding on the ground together. Being reluctant fliers they crowd close together, even in the breeding season, rather than move to a new colony. This means that their feeding ground tends to be fairly close to the roost, preferably within walking distance.

The Canada feeds on a variety of grasses, grazing on nearby farmland, arable and pasture, and marshes. They are daytime feeders, although their times of movement are more erratic than other species of geese. With their long bills the birds are adept at stripping seed from the stems of plants and probing in marshy ground for roots. Their diet is basically vegetable and in common with other species of geese they have adapted their feeding habits to take full advantage of modern agriculture, feeding on cereals, grasses, roots and tubers.

The population of Canada geese has increased dramatically since the 1950s and is still growing. The first census of Canadas was taken in July 1953, when it was thought there were around 3,500 birds in Britain. The next census was in 1967 and 1968, when it appeared that the numbers had risen to around 10,500. The population now stands at around 20,000.

The recommended shot size for this goose is 1 or 3.

DABBLING DUCK

Mallard (*Anas platyrhynchos*)

The best-known and most widespread duck in Britain is undoubt-edly the mallard, the most readily distinguishable being the drake. It is the duck that has adapted well to all environments, with tame mallard common in almost every city park pond, eagerly scrabbling for bread and left-over picnics thrown by visitors. Conversely, the truly 'wild' mallards found in this country, although excellent sport for the wildfowler, are wary birds that take flight at the first suspicion of danger.

The resident mallard population remains static, although large numbers of migrant birds arrive during the autumn months (September and October) to augment the population. These birds come mainly from Western Europe and Iceland to winter in Britain, and return to their breeding grounds in April or May.

Mallard are found in virtually every wet area that could possibly hold a duck. It likes shallow water where it can feed on underwater plants and prefers inland waterways in general.

As with all the duck family it is the male that has the distinct colouring and more striking appearance. It is a beautiful duck with a glossy green velvety head, white dog collar and brown breast, with curly black feathers on its upper tail. The female mallard on the other hand, is a rather dull brown. Both birds have a blue wing patch.

When moulting the drake loses his beautifully coloured plumage and takes on the brownish hue of the female, although he is slightly darker. This occurs during the period July to September, when the ducks are said to be in eclipse. During this period of moulting the drake is vulnerable to predators which explains his more subdued coloration.

The male is slightly larger than the female and weighs 1,000–1,450 g, averaging 1,200 g. The female weighs from 900–1,350 g and averages 1,000 g. The mallard is the largest of Britain's dabbling (surface feeding) ducks.

Being a dabbler means that the mallard has a broad, shovel-like bill which is perfectly adapted to filter food from the water. It does not dive for food and prefers shallow water so that when not scooping food from the surface it can up-end itself and reach the vegetation growing on the bottom of a pond.

Opposite The wildfowler's dream – Canadas coming in during early evening flight.

This painting, *First Arrivals*, wonderfully captures the 'feel' of morning flight as the mallard come in.

The diet of the mallard is varied and it adapts its feeding pattern to its environment. The foods it takes consist mainly of water plants and marginal seeds, although the adults prefer cereals such as barley and wheat and during the autumn will fly considerable distances to feed on stubble. Mallard are night feeders, roosting on water during the day and flighting into fields of cereals and other farmland to feed. They return to the water at dawn to roost.

The mallard selects a mate late in the year, with the males courting a female by swimming around her in a wide circle, with neck stretched out along the surface. It is also common during this time to see male mallards flying after a single female. It is thought that once a mate has been selected, they remain with each other for life. The breeding pair fly off together to the breeding grounds early in the year, from February onwards.

The loudest and most typical 'quack, quack, quack' of duck on a pond invariably comes from mallard, and it is the female that makes this distinctive sound. The male makes a softer, more subdued 'quork' or 'quek', particularly when alarmed or suspicious.

The resident mallard population in Britain is thought to be in the region of 100,000 to 150,000 pairs, with the winter visitors bringing the numbers up to around 300,000. The population numbers for the whole of Western Europe (including the UK) is thought to number many millions.

Mallard provide excellent sport for the wildfowler, being easy to decoy onto water and to call with a duck call. When flighting at night on a pond, or in early morning when visibility is restricted, an excellent guide to identification is the whistling of the mallard's wings, which can also tell you from which direction they are approaching.

At night duck will often make a first pass over the pond where they intend to land. If birds are approaching on the high side it is wise to let them pass. They are likely to fly around in a circle for a second, lower run to the water. This habit is more likely to be observed in areas where the birds have been shot at and disturbed.

The mallard is one of the few birds of which the sportsman can, if he is fortunate enough to be set up under a good flight, shoot several without feeling that he is decimating their number. The mallard is truly the fowler's bird.

The recommended shot size for this duck is 5 or 6.

Wigeon (*Anas penelope*)

The wigeon is slightly smaller than the mallard and has been a breeding resident of Britain for only a relatively short time. The first recorded nesting site was in Sutherland in the north of Scotland, in the early nineteenth century. The birds have expanded in number since then, although they have not established themselves to any great degree outside Scotland.

The wigeon is an Arctic to sub-Arctic breeding duck. Although the resident breeding population of wigeon is estimated to be only about 500 pairs mostly found in Scotland on Loch Leven, the winter population of birds is swollen to well over 200,000 by a vast influx of visitors arriving in Britain from Iceland, Russia and Scandinavia.

Because of the relatively mild climatic conditions experienced in Britain the country gets nearly half of the entire wigeon population of northwest Europe. They arrive in late September to early November, and as the weather turns colder will gradually move towards the south of the country. Wigeon generally prefer shallow freshwater areas, although they can be found in rivers and even on coastal marshes.

The adult male has a pale golden crown on a chestnut head, and a white wing patch which is easily identified in flight. The female is of a uniformly brown colour, with a high forehead and a small bill. She is smaller than the female mallard, with a more pointed tail. Both male and female have bright green wing patches. The immature male is easily distinguished by the lack of a white shoulder patch. Both sexes are of similar size. The male weighs 650–1,050 g, averaging 850 g, and the female weighs 600–900 g, averaging 775 g.

Both sexes go into the moulting eclipse around July, when the male loses any bright colouring and becomes a dark brown version of the female.

Wigeon are gregarious birds with large flocks numbering into the hundreds commonly seen as they move along the estuaries and mudflats of our coasts. They spend the day resting on the estuaries, flighting inland to feed at dusk, and returning to the coasts at dawn. However, in areas where they are not disturbed the wigeon can be seen feeding during the day. When disturbed the flock will rise straight out of the water and remain in a tight formation as they fly quickly away. Although a dabbling duck, the wigeon feeds, like geese, by grazing and eating grass or mudflat plants.

The call of the male wigeon is the familiar 'whee-oo', similar to a whistling kettle, which will be answered by other males in the flock. The female sound is a gentle purr.

Being gregarious birds wigeon can be drawn into decoys, but as an added incentive to bring them down the serious fowler who is likely to find himself in a position where wigeon will show up should add the whistle from a whistling kettle to his bag of gear. A little practice can soon make experts of even the most tone deaf amongst us, and I have found, as with so many other species of wildfowl, that the combination of sound and sight often brings about success.

The recommended shot size for this duck is 5 or 6.

Teal (*Anas crecca*)

The teal is a beautiful little duck with distinctive markings on its head. It is small and very agile, springing almost vertically into the air when disturbed. It is, indeed, this agility in flight that gives the teal its reputation as a highly sporting bird.

Although teal are found throughout Britain, the resident breeding population is fairly limited, but increases dramatically with winter visitors and passage migrants. It is estimated that about half the winter population of Europe is found in Britain. The passage birds and winter residents come from Iceland, Scandinavia and other parts of Northern Europe, arriving earlier than most migrants in August to October. The main concentrations of resident birds are in Scotland, Ireland and the north and east of England.

Teal generally prefer freshwater ponds in moorland country, although they do frequent the coastal waters and mudflats. Being a typical dabbling duck it does not like deep water where it cannot reach the vegetation growing at the bottom. Unfortunately for the teal, these shallow waters are usually amongst the first to freeze over in winter. In harsh weather therefore the teal will leave their moorland sites and congregate on the estuaries and mudflats.

The teal is the smallest of the native British ducks. The male has grey upper parts and a chestnut head, with a distinctive metallic green eye patch surrounded by a thin band of yellow, and a white stripe above the wing. The female is a dull brown. Both sexes have a metallic black and green wing patch.

In flight the black and green patches are visible in both sexes, as are the black and yellow undertail feathers of the female. Both male and female are in eclipse during July or August, resuming full plumage around September. Males weigh from 325–375 g and females 260–325 g.

One of the most interesting behavioural aspects of the teal is its tremendous aerial agility. Outside the breeding season tightly packed flocks of teal can be seen wheeling through the sky like waders. When danger threatens the teal have the ability to spring into the air almost vertically, flying away with a twisting, swerving flight.

Teal are gregarious birds and are usually found in flocks, some quite large, although the flocks have no set formation and the birds are tightly packed in irregular groups.

Typical of the dabbling duck, the teal eats as it swims, or walks in the shallows, scooping up plants with its bill. Occasionally it will up-end to pull up deeper plants. Teal are basically water-plant eaters, eating both the plant and its seeds, but will also feed on insects, worms and molluscs.

The drake has a distinctive and most unusual voice, a musical, ringing-like 'shring-shring', although the sound made by the female is more duck-like, being a high-pitched 'quack' which she will make when alarmed. The call of the male is often heard being repeated throughout a flock as they wheel about overhead.

Estimates vary widely on the numbers of breeding teal there are in Britain. Although widely distributed they are spread thinly over the country and the resident birds possibly number as few as 300 pairs, up to 7,000. Their numbers are of course increased dramatically during the autumn and winter, when around 100,000 teal inhabit the country.

Not for nothing do the clay pigeon enthusiasts have one of their more daunting targets named the springing teal, for this super little bird can quite literally jump from the water when disturbed and rise at what seems quite astonishing speed. The combination of its tiny size and swift movement results in the teal being an extremely challenging bird. Few shooters are able to grasp just how fast the bird is flying, particularly when flighting in the evening when any advance visual warning of the birds' approach is less likely.

The recommended shot size for teal is 6 or 7.

Pintail (*Anas acuta*)

Often described as our most elegant duck, the pintail, as its name suggests, has a distinctive long tail. The male has two central tail feathers which grow into a sharp point up to 15 cm long. Although distribution of the pintail in this country is spread thinly, pintail probably have the highest world-wide population of any duck, particularly in North America, where there are large numbers across the entire continent.

Few pintail spend more than the winter months in Britain. It is thought that the resident breeding population numbers only about 50 pairs. The pintail tends to be a restless breeder, rarely using the same site for longer than two years, and this makes accurate counting difficult. The few birds that breed in Britain are scattered throughout the country and Ireland.

The birds that come here to winter are from Iceland, northern Europe and Scandinavia. These winter visitors arrive in September or October and return to their breeding grounds in April. They stick to the estuaries and mudflats rather than travel inland to fresh water, and concentrations of pintail can be found on many estuaries around our coasts.

A pintail.

The pintail is unmistakable, with its long tail feathers. Even the female has elongated tail feathers, although not nearly as long as the male's. It is a long slender duck with an elegance both on water and in the air. The adult male is light grey in colour, with a chocolate and white head, white breast and bronze wing patch. The wings of this duck, when seen in flight, are long and pointed. The female pintail is speckled brown, a slender creature with long pointed wings and a steel grey bill. Both sexes go into eclipse from July to October and both sexes are of approximately the same size. The birds weigh 600–750 g.

Considered to be the fastest flying of our duck, the pintail flies with a rapid movement and will usually be the first in a mixed group of duck to take flight when danger approaches. They gather in flocks, sometimes flying in an uneven V formation similar to geese. They also feed in flocks. Pintail not only swim gracefully they also walk with an ease unusual in duck.

Being a dabbling duck, the pintail feeds on the surface of the water and up-ends to reach the bottom of shallow pools. Its diet consists mainly of water plants, although it will also take insects, molluscs and worms. They flight into stubble at night to feed on the grain, leaving their coastal roosts at dusk and returning again at dawn. Unlike most other duck pintail feed at night by choice, even where they suffer little disturbance.

Although widespread throughout the world, the pintail is the rarest of the dabbling ducks resident in Britain. Even with the influx of passage migrants and winter visitors, the number rarely tops the 20,000 mark.

The recommended shot size for this duck is 5 or 6.

Gadwall (*Anas strepera*)

The scarcest of the ducks on the game list, whether breeding or as a winter visitor, is the gadwall. It is, however, distributed widely on a world-wide scale – nearly 200,000 birds are thought to reside in the USSR. Unlike most other duck the male gadwall is not highly coloured or distinctively marked. However, he is still an attractive bird with softly coloured plumage and splashes of colour on the wings.

Just over a hundred years ago (1850) a pair of gadwall was caught and wing clipped and then released onto the Breckland Meres in East Anglia. There they started breeding and the small population which now breed in this country are probably descended from that pair, for before this occurred the gadwall was known only as a passage bird or a winter visitor.

The gadwall is still a sparse breeder, the colonies in England – in East Anglia and the surrounding areas – being made up of feral birds descended from the original pair. However, small breeeding colonies have been established around Loch Leven in Scotland and in Ireland. The Scottish and Irish birds are more likely to be part of the natural expansion of the gadwall descended from East European, Scandinavian and Icelandic stock.

The gadwall likes shallow fresh water, with plenty of vegetation and cover. It is a typical dabbling duck although it is vegetarian except for the first week of its life. As a duckling it will feed on insects, worms and snails, since they are rich in protein. It takes leaves, seeds, plants and weeds. It is known to graze occasionally on stubble, feeding at night in areas where it is disturbed. If left alone it feeds during the day, although it moves about frequently from roost to feeding grounds.

Both male and female gadwall are of subdued colouring, the

drake being a grey brown and the duck of a similar colour to the female mallard although she is slightly smaller. Both duck and drake have a distinctive white wing patch which is unlike that of any other duck. The presence of the wing patch on the female gadwall helps to distinguish it from the mallard. The male has a reddish brown and black patch on the wing with black tail coverts. In flight the wing patches are easily discernible as are the sharp pointed wings. The gadwall starts its annual eclipse earlier than most ducks, from June to late August.

The gadwall is a shy and wary duck that congregates in small flocks only, seldom in large groups. It can move about confidently on land and can often be seen scrounging about on marshy vegetation. In flight it has a rapid wing movement, although it does not fly as fast as the mallard. Like all duck it is an agile swimmer and it sits in an upright position, holding its wings and tail high out of the water.

The sounds made by the male gadwall are a deep-throated 'whek', which sounds more like a croak or a grunt, and a whistling sound. The female call is a soft duck-like quack.

The resident breeding population of gadwall in Britain is thought to be no more than 300 pairs, with the average autumn/winter population being between 2,000 and 3,000. Whilst the bird's international population is healthy, there are few in Britain. The gadwall therefore falls into the category that requires a responsible attitude from sportsmen. Whilst it is entirely legal to shoot the bird and it is delicious to eat, the sportsman should practice a certain restraint. Personally I would not consider lifting my gun to any species with so few numbers, when there are so many more numerous species on the game list. On the other hand this is entirely a personal view and it is up to the individual fowler to make his own decisions.

The recommended shot size for this duck is 5 or 6.

Shoveler (*Anas clypeata*)

As its name suggests, the most distinctive feature of the shoveler is its large shovel-like bill, which is common to both sexes. It is an unmistakable identification mark, even in flight. The bill is longer than the head — about 9 cm long — and is rounded at the end. Although the long flat bill gives the shoveler a slightly comical look, the male is an attractive duck with a bright green head, similar in colour to the male mallard.

In many parts of Britain, the shoveler is one of the rarer dabbling duck. There is a small resident breeding population, but its thin distribution is due to the relative scarcity of its favoured habitat — marsh or shallow muddy waters as are found in lowland areas such as East Anglia. Their numbers are unlikely to increase because of land reclamation and the drainage of wetland.

The shoveler is not common in Scotland, the land being generally too high, with few marshy areas for the duck to frequent. Because they are dabbling ducks the shoveler will not go into deep water but prefers shallows where its scoop-like bill can shovel up food from the surface. Winter visitors arrive from September to November, with the resident birds leaving during October. The shoveler returns to its breeding ground early, and will begin to depart as early as February or March.

The broad bill of this duck is its most distinctive feature, although there are other aspects to look for when identifying the shoveler. The male has a lovely metallic green head like the mallard, with a white breast and chestnut belly. In flight its prominent blue shoulder patches, the white bar and the green rear patch on the wing can be seen. The female also has the blue wing patch, although hers is a duller blue. She has a brown head and body with speckled underparts — and of course the large bill. Both sexes go into eclipse though that of the male may be prolonged — he can start around June and not regain his normal plumage until December, although this is not common. The average weight of the shoveler, both male and female, falls between 500–700 g.

The shoveler feeds on both vegetable and animal matter, including insects, freshwater molluscs, seeds, plants and weed. In areas where the shoveler is being disturbed it will feed after dusk, although if left undisturbed it will feed both during the day and at night.

The shoveler does not congregate in huge flocks, rather it stays in small groups when feeding, although large numbers can be found in one place when roosting. It is a wary duck that generally stays out of the way of man, keeping to the middle of a waterway when there is any suspicion that something may be amiss.

A quiet bird, the shoveler is usually unheard outside the breeding season. During courtship flight it is common to hear the male utter a hoarse 'took-took' sound as he chases his mate through the air. The female replies with a duck-like 'quack quack', similar to the mallard.

The resident breeding population of shovelers is thought to number about 1,000 pairs, and with winter visitors and passing migrants arriving in late autumn the average number of duck found in Britain is around 6,000–7,000.

Shovelers are not difficult birds to shoot, being slower in flight than the mallard, although the erratic line they take as they appear to zig-zag and jink can make them challenging. However, since their flesh is less desirable than other duck on the game list, the fowler should try one on the table first before shooting any quantity.

The recommended shot size for this duck is 5 or 6.

DIVING DUCK

Diving duck differ from the dabblers in that instead of dabbling about on the surface of the water to feed and up-ending occasionally, they submerge their entire body as they dive underwater, sometimes to a fair depth, to pick up plants and animal matter from the bottom of a lake or other waterway. Consequently the diving duck will tend to frequent deeper waters than most dabblers.

Tufted duck (*Aythya fuligula*)

Although completely unknown as a breeding bird in Britain until the early 1800s, the tufted duck has established itself so well that it is now the most common diving duck found in Britain. Like the mallard it has adapted its habits and habitat to live in city parks and other urban ponds. In this type of location the tuftie is a fairly tame bird, joining the scramble for scraps of bread. In the wild, however, they are wary birds that will dive at the first hint of danger.

The distribution of the tufted duck spans the whole of the North European and Asian continents, the birds preferring large stretches of water, although it will also happily frequent smaller areas.

The British population of tufted duck during the winter is swollen by the arrival of migrants from Iceland and northern Europe from September to the end of November. It is unusual to spot the arrival of these visitors because they move during the hours of darkness. They return to their breeding ground between late February and early May.

The male tufted duck is easy to identify, even at distance, by its white flanks and tuft of feathers protruding from the back of his skull, which is a velvety purple black. In flight he shows a white bar across the wing. The female is a rather dull brown colour and can be mistaken for a female scaup (not on the game list). She too has a tuft of feathers on the back of her head, although this is not as pronounced as the male's. Her wings have the same white bar across the upper parts. The eclipse runs from July to October. The male and female are the same size and weight, around 700 g.

In common with most diving ducks, the tuftie will dive to escape from danger rather than take flight. When it does rise from the water it lets its feet drop, hitting the surface as it rises. The tuftie is probably the most able of the diving ducks and can submerge itself for at least a minute in waters up to about 2 metres in depth. When diving the duck will pick up both animal and vegetable matter, although it prefers animal – molluscs, insects, tadpoles, etc.

The tufted duck is a gregarious bird, with parties of a few dozen commonly seen, although they sometimes congregate in large flocks and can often be seen mixing with pochards and coots.

Outside the breeding season the tufted duck is a fairly quiet bird, not given to making a loud noise, although the female will sometimes give out a low growl when alarmed.

It is estimated that around 7,000 pairs of tufted ducks breed in Britain, with the number increasing. This is swollen by the arrival of the winter visitors in late autumn, when there can be up to 50,000 ducks in the country.

Shooting tufted duck is not exhilarating, unless flighting coming into a waterway. Unlike teal who can spring out of a reed bed during a rough shoot, the tuftie does not rise in a particularly sporting fashion, their take off being more laborious and slow.

The recommended shot size for this duck is 5 or 6.

Goldeneye (*Bucephala clangula*)

The goldeneye is found in the northern hemisphere right around the globe, but there are no birds in Greenland or Iceland. They winter on any large waterway, inland or coastal, south of the

A pair of goldeneye.

breeding range. The winter visitors that arrive in Britain from September to November are mostly from Scandinavia, with a few arriving from northern Russia. They prefer the coastal areas and estuaries unlike the other two diving duck on the game list.

Although as its name suggests this bird has a prominent golden eye, this is not its most distinctive feature. The adult male appears to be basically a black and white bird with a curious square-shaped head. The head has a greenish sheen to it, with a high forehead and short bill, giving the appearance of being rectangular. The male also has a white circle on his cheek, below the eye. The female is greyish white, with a brown head and white collar and is a similar shape to the male. Both sexes have rectangular white wing patches, which are clearly visible in flight. The eclipse for the goldeneye, both sexes, is normally between August and October. Male and female goldeneye are the same size and weight, 700–900 g.

The goldeneye is usually seen in small parties, being less gregarious than most ducks, although occasionally large parties can be seen over Scottish waters. It prefers to remain with its own species and it is rare to see goldeneye mingle with other ducks, although they may be on the same waterway.

The goldeneye has a fast wing action in flight, flying strongly and easily. When in flight the wings produce a distinctive whistling sound which is unmistakable.

The bulk of the goldeneye diet is animal, and is made up of insects, tadpoles, small fish, molluscs and shrimps, although water plants are also eaten. It dives under the surface to feed and will sometimes swim underwater rather than on the surface.

The goldeneye rarely makes a sound although the duck can utter a low growling grunt. When the ducks are excited they will puff out their chests and heads to show excitement rather than vocalize.

Although only a few pairs breed in Britain, with the dramatic influx of migratory visitors the winter population of these birds is quite healthy and numbers over 10,000, with a European total of around 150,000 birds.

The goldeneye is a more challenging bird to shoot than any other diving duck, since it rises more rapidly when disturbed and certainly can be challenging shooting when flighting in. However, I would recommend restraint, since the flesh is not succulent and is an acquired taste. Unless you enjoy them on the table there is little justification in shooting this species.

The recommended shot size for this duck is 5 or 6.

Pochard (*Aythya ferina*)

The pochard is often seen in city parks enjoying the scraps of food thrown by visitors. However, it has never really established itself as a breeder in any great number. Indeed it was rare to find a breeding pair of pochards before the last century, when they were thought to be confined to the East Anglia area. Although they are now found in most parts of Britain, the bulk of the population is in the south and east of England.

The small British population of pochards is augmented by the arrival of migrants from northern Europe and Siberia. These birds favour large stretches of inland waters in England and Scotland and soon disperse to their preferred sites after arrival, returning to their breeding grounds in March or April. The resident birds usually remain in the country, although they may move to a different part and sometimes will fly south to the Mediterranean in severe weather.

The most distinctive feature of the male pochard is its lovely brick red head, contrasting with its black breast and grey back. Although it may be mistaken for the cock wigeon, the male pochard has no bright cream head or white wing bars. The female pochard is a dull brown colour with pale face markings, particularly around her bill, and is streaked lightly on her back and sides. She may be confused with the female tufted duck but unlike the tuftie the female pochard has no white wing bar. Both male and female pochard have grey wing bars, easily spotted when in flight. The male will be in eclipse between July and September. The female has no eclipse plumage. Both male and female are the same size and weight, averaging 850 g.

Pochard are gregarious birds and it is common to see them densely packed together on the water. It spends most of its time in the water, where like all diving ducks, it will dive for its food, although pochards will on occasion up-end in the style of the dabbling duck. The pochard prefers a more vegetarian diet, which consists mainly of roots, seeds and other water plants.

When danger threatens the pochard it will not readily take flight, preferring to swim from the threat or dive. In fact the pochard is rather slow and ungainly at take off as it has to run across the surface of the water like a coot before getting airborne, with wings beating rapidly to give it height.

To shoot duck a good retriever is essential. This black labrador holds a mallard duck.

The resident population of pochard is thought to number no more than about 350–450 pairs. With visiting migrants these figures swell to reach the 35,000 mark.

As with the tufted duck the pochard is not an inspiring bird to shoot, other than in flighting, when it can be quite difficult.

The recommended shot size for this duck is 5 or 6.

OTHER WATERFOWL

Moorhen (*Gallinula chloropus*)

The moorhen is not in any way connected with moors or moorland as its name might suggest. The 'moor' comes from an Anglo-Saxon word 'mor' meaning mere or lake, so the name is actually as form of 'merehen' or 'bird of the lakes'. The moorhen can be found on just about any stretch of water, big or small, throughout the whole of Britain. This bird of the lakes does not have webbed feet although it is as at home on the water as any waterfowl. The resident British population of moorhens is swollen in the winter with migrant birds arriving from Europe.

It is rare to find moorhen near salt water – they seem to stick to freshwater areas, even when food is scarce. They are less fussy about where they live than the coot, with which they are often confused, and will take to any wet or boggy spot.

The moorhen is of a dark brown and black coloration with a conspicuous vivid red forehead, which extends down to its bill, the tip of which is yellow. The bird has white undertail feathers, with the male and female moorhen being identical in size and coloration, weighing about 425 g. The juvenile moorhen is a duller brown than its parent with no red flashes on its face. The chicks are black with a blue crown, and again no red flashes, unlike coot chicks which, conversely, do have bright red heads.

The moorhen is a shy bird which seldom enjoys the company of even its own species. It will aggressively defend its own territory and disputes over boundaries can cause injury. It can submerge itself in water when alarmed, save for the tip of its bill which it leaves protruding. It manages to do this by expelling air from air sacs in its plumage and treading water.

It is not a bird that takes to flight easily and will only fly if it is left no other choice. When it does take off, flight is laboured and low, with the legs left dangling.

The call of the moorhen is a croaking sound, 'kurruk' and 'kittic', which is often heard at night. The moorhen eats such a variety of foods that it can sometimes be a pest, eating not only fruits, seeds and sown crops, but also the eggs and chicks of other birds. They can damage cress beds and other crops more severely than other birds by uprooting the whole plant.

The estimated population of moorhen in the country range from 300,000 pairs to nearly 1 million.

Moorhen are not really shot by fowlers, although they are probably one of the first water birds shot by young guns. They are completely uninspiring as sporting birds since their flight is slow and cumbersome. Whilst the flesh is edible it does not compare to the more succulent flesh of the other waterfowl on the game list.

Coot (*Fulica atra*)

The coot and the moorhen are often confused with one another, many people having the impression that the birds are one and the same, with only regional variations in name. Although they are of roughly the same general coloration and live in similar habitats, the two birds are different species and the wildfowler should be able to spot the differences between the two.

The coot is found throughout Britain, with some visiting birds arriving to winter in Britain. Although found in all parts of the country it is less common in northwest Scotland and some of the islands. More fastidious in its choice of habitat than the moorhen, the coot prefers larger expanses of water, with plenty of reed and tall grasses to give it security. When the weather is inclement the coot will move to the coasts and estuaries. It is found in a variety of water areas from parks to such unlikely places as mature flooded gravel pits where the birds can dive for the aquatic plants that make up the bulk of its diet.

The coot is all black, except for a white patch on its forehead known as the frontal shield, which extends down to its white bill, hence the origin of the phrase 'bald as a coot'. It also has narrow white wing bars, but these are only seen when the bird is in flight. The sexes are alike in size and coloration, an adult coot weighing approximately 800 g. The juvenile coot is greyer than

The result of a superb morning's flight.

the young moorhen with plain grey throat and breast. The chicks have brightly coloured heads, distinct from the moorhen chicks which have blue heads.

Coots can be aggressive birds and will guard their territories jealously, males frequently fighting and squabbling over their boundaries. These squabbles can be particularly fierce during the breeding season. During the winter months coots become more social and often form large flocks on open stretches of water.

Like the moorhen, the coot can submerge itself almost completely, leaving only its bill protruding from the water. It does not readily take flight and when it does it patttters along the water to take off, flying low with its great long legs trailing behind.

When feeding it will dive under the water to pick up a piece of vegetation and then bob back to the surface in exactly the same spot, just like a cork, where it eats the food. Water plants and shoots form the bulk of the coot's diet, although it will take water insects and very occasionally chicks and eggs from other birds.

The population numbers considerably less than the moorhen, with an estimated 100,000 pairs resident in the country.

Few British sportsmen would lift their gun to a coot, its flesh, unless it has been feeding on grasses and grains, tending to have a strong earthy taste. However, I would advise all sportsmen to discover for themselves whether they enjoy a coot on the table, for it is on the game list and if properly cooked, some people may find it quite tasty.

CHAPTER EIGHT

Preparing the Game

I believe that, with the exception of vermin species, anything that the sportsman is likely to shoot he should be prepared to eat. In addition, I believe that no one can truly call himself a sportsman until he is capable of performing every aspect of the job, from shooting through to the table.

This is probably a result of my shooting background, when as a teenager with my single barrel I had to work hard for any game I caught. Rabbits were the staple with a few hares and even less frequently a pheasant or duck. I shot them for sport, but also as an integral part of the sport I skinned or plucked the game for the table and took great pleasure in concocting, much to my mother's inconvenience, quite elaborate dishes.

Skinning all game is best done in a game larder where the facilities exist to hose down floors, wash working surfaces and hang game in a fly-free environment. This, however, is a luxury few have access to. As a second choice I prefer to skin and clean game outdoors. This is fine if you live in the country, although working outdoors is really only feasible during winter, since in the summer flies quickly appear. Most people end up skinning and cleaning small game in the kitchen.

SMALL GAME

The technique of cleaning and preparing small game is the same whether it is a squirrel, rabbit or hare. Lay the carcass on its back on the work surface (preferably the draining board). Pucker the skin with your thumb and forefinger and with a sharp knife cut a small piece of skin away so that you can get your fingers underneath. Take care not to burst the stomach wall. Work the skin away and cut only where necessary. I prefer to skin small game almost entirely by hand, pulling the skin away from the carcass. Skin the animal down below the joint where you are going to remove the feet. Cut through the joint. (Practice will soon enable you to cut through with surgical accuracy.) Cut the tail off at the base, leaving it attached to the skin, then pull the skin up over the neck. It's very much like removing an outer garment. Cut through the neck. You then have the skin with feet, head and tail attached, separate from the carcass.

With the carcass still on its back, now cut the abdominal wall from sternum to pelvis and with your fingers remove all the innards from the windpipe down to its pelvis, taking care when cutting through at the pelvis that you don't allow the contents of the bladder to spill on to the meat. Split the pelvis on the under side and remove the anal tract. There you have the carcass ready for washing under cold running water to remove any hairs or dirt.

Personally I prefer to skin small game in a different way. I simply pucker the skin on the animal's back, cutting through and then grip the skin with both hands and pull. In this manner the skin comes off the animal in two halves, like a sweater and trousers. Cleaning out the animal's innards is done as above.

Whichever method you try, use a sharp knife and with a little practice you will be surprised how simple skinning and cleaning is.

LARGE GAME

Large game is cleaned in basically the same way, the principal difference being that due to the size of a large game animal such as a deer and the possibility of spoiling the meat, the contents of the chest and the intestines are removed on site after the animal has been shot. To clean (gralloch) a deer lay it on its back with its hind quarters downhill. Pucker the skin on the belly. Use the tip of your blade carefully to make a small incision in the skin, ensuring that you cut through the skin only. Push two fingers through the hole, using them to hold down the intestines. Then with the tip of your knife between both fingertips, carefully cut the animal from sternum to crutch. Take care that it is only the skin that you are cutting — avoid cutting through the abdominal wall. When you have made the incision in the skin, it may be necessary to start peeling the skin back by freeing it with your knife, but normally it is a relatively simple matter, even with very large deer, to free the skin from the carcass using your hands.

In the case of roe deer I prefer to separate the skin from the carcass, from the animal's neck to its pelvis, around its torso, indeed as much of the carcass as possible, whilst still leaving the skin attached to the body, with the only incision being the original one from sternum to crutch. By freeing the skin in this fashion it allows me to hang the carcass in the larder until I wish to butcher it. Then by simply making a few cuts in the skin, it falls away.

Once you have freed the skin back from the incision you will be faced with the large smooth abdominal wall. Carefully make a small incision, using the tip of your knife and put the tips of both fingers through the abdominal wall in the same fashion as described for the skin. Then, taking care not to cut through any intestines, cut the abdominal wall from sternum to crutch. You will find that once you have made the incision large enough to put your hand in, it is easier to hold the intestines down.

The muscle wall which separates the chest cavity from the intestines is the diaphragm. In small species of deer this is easily punctured with your fingers. In large species it will require cutting. Cut through it and holding the back of your hand (without the knife) inside the chest cavity against the sternum, push your arm in, until you find the animal's windpipe. Take a firm grip. Now taking care not to cut your arm, put your knife hand into the chest. I normally put the knife in reversed, turning it only *in situ*. The idea is that whilst you hold the windpipe in your left hand you cut through with your right. Remove the knife, lay it aside, then taking the windpipe in both hands, pull. You should remove all the innards, down to the pelvis, cutting through the anal tract. Retrieve heart, liver and kidneys from the gralloch.

Alternatively take out only the intestines and associated organs, leaving the chest contents intact for later removal.

The carcass is then transported and hung in the larder, or in winter outdoors. Remove the head, and feet at the hocks. Hang the animal by its hind legs. The best and simplest method is to put a wooden stave (e.g. a thick broom handle) through an

Opposite As the last illustration in this book it is appropriate to show a non-game species, for the true sportsman values all wildlife and is privileged to share and preserve their world and wild places. What creature more than all others represents the majesty of the wilderness than the golden eagle?

incision between the bone and Achilles tendon in both hind legs and to hoist the animal well clear of the ground and any vermin. Split the pelvis, removing the contents. Then split the animal straight through the sternum to the throat using a saw and prop the chest cavity open with a peg.

The purpose of hanging is to tenderize the meat and temperature is vital. An animal hung for two or three days in summer could be soured and inedible, whereas an animal hung in the middle of winter could remain for several weeks without detriment to the meat. What must be avoided when hanging is the carcass getting wet, so if you are hanging your carcass outdoors it must be under a roof. Experience alone will teach you how long you like your game hung. Personally, I find that a week in a cold (not frozen) temperature is sufficient.

When you wish to butcher the carcass, give yourself plenty of time so that you can do a neat, unhurried job. Remove the skin, then since your animal is hanging head down, remove both forelegs at the shoulder which may be boned and rolled, boned

Hinds in the heather. Hind carcasses are preferable meat to that of stags.

and cubed for stew, or left intact and roasted on the bone.

Remove the neck. This is best used for boiling.

The area from the top of the saddle, i.e. where the bottom rib joins the spine to between the shoulder blades, can be boned out giving two long fillets. Alternatively, by removing the lower part of the ribs for soup or spare ribs (with smaller species of deer there is not sufficient flesh on the ribs for anything other than stock), the long fillets on the upper parts of the back can be used as chops, by splitting the spine and cutting through between each rib.

The carcass will now have been reduced to two haunches and the best part of the saddle. On either side of the spine on the upper part of the saddle are the two fillets known as the sirloins. On the underpart of the spine, the two small muscles are the fillets. These can be removed for frying or left on the bone and roasted. Remove the saddle where it joins the pelvis. This now leaves you the two haunches attached at the pelvis. Cut them through from the underside into the ball joint and up, following the bone to retain as much meat as possible on the haunch. Discard the pelvis.

Remove the lower part of the limb at the joint, using the flesh for mincing, stewing, etc.

The upper part of the limb, the haunch, can be roasted whole or cut into roasts, depending on its size. Haunch meat can be fried or roasted.

GAME BIRDS

Game birds may be hung, although waterfowl should not be hung for more than a few days. It is the practice with some individuals to skin birds. By doing so you make preparation much easier and of course remove much of the fat. It is really a lazy way of preparing the bird, and should only be done if, for instance, the skin is badly damaged, making plucking difficult. If the skin is so badly torn that it will not look good, even after careful plucking, then it may as well be skinned. Birds skinned never look good as a carcass for presentation and much of the flavour and moisture is lost. Therefore, plucking is by far the best method of bird preparation.

Unlike hair, which grows uniformly all over a body, feathers grow in feather tracts. The best method of cleaning a bird is to lay it with its head away from you, then holding it with your left hand, grasp one or two feathers with your right and smartly pull them out. The secret is to pluck only a few feathers at a time, not a bunch. The adhesion to the carcass will be greater and there is a much higher chance of pulling a hole in the skin, particularly with fatter birds. Pluck the bird completely, always taking care to pluck the feathers beyond where you wish to make a cut on the wing and neck.

When you have plucked the bird completely, remove the wings, feet and head. Then draw the bird by making an incision in the stomach and clean it out entirely from windpipe to anus, taking care to ensure that the lungs are removed.

Remove the crop, which can be packed full or almost empty, by separating it from the skin with your fingers. Gradually work it free from the carcass and pull it out intact. If you are too heavy handed and the crop membrane bursts, just remove it and the contents as best you can. Rinse it out.

Rinse the bird out thoroughly in cold running water and place it somewhere for the water to drain out of it before cooking or freezing.

APPENDIX

Shooting Seasons

GAME AND WILDFOWL

Grouse (England, Scotland, Wales)	Aug 12 – Dec 10
Grouse (N. Ireland)	Aug 12 – Nov 30
Grouse (Eire)	Sept 1 – Sep 30
Black grouse	Aug 1 – Dec 10
Capercaillie (Scotland only)	Oct 1 – Jan 31
Ptarmigan (Scotland only)	Aug 12 – Dec 10
Pheasant (see note 5)	Oct 1 – Feb 1
Pheasant (Eire)	Nov 1 – Jan 31
Grey partridge (England, Scotland, Wales) (see note 6)	Sep 1 – Feb 1
Grey partridge (Eire)	Nov 1 – Nov 15
Redlegged partridge (see note 7)	Sept 1 – Feb 1
Woodcock (England, Wales, N. Ireland)	Oct 1 – Jan 31
Woodcock (Scotland)	Sept 1 – Jan 31
Woodcock (Eire)	Nov 1 – Jan 31

Snipe (England, Scotland, Wales)	Aug 12 – Jan 31
Snipe (N. Ireland)	Oct 1 – Jan 31
Snipe (Eire)	Sept 1 – Jan 31
Golden plover	Sept 1 – Jan 31
Wildfowl (ducks, geese, coot, moorhen)	Sept 1 – Jan 31

NOTES

1   All dates are inclusive.

2   The law relating to shooting applies only during daylight hours. In Scotland, England and Wales only rabbits and hares may be shot at night. No other game may be shot at night. It is illegal to shoot at night in N. Ireland.

3   There is no close season for hare but hare cannot be sold from 1 March to 31 July.

4   There is no close season for woodpigeon.

5   In Ireland, both north and south of the border, special licences must be obtained in order to shoot hen pheasants.

6   In N. Ireland the grey partridge is protected.

7   In N. Ireland a licence must be obtained before redlegged partridge may be shot. In Eire the bird is protected.

DEER

Stags/bucks (England, Wales, N. Ireland)	May 1 – Jul 31
Stags/bucks (Scotland)	Oct 21 – Jun 30
Stags/bucks (Eire)	Mar 1 – Aug 31
Hinds/does (England, Scotland, N. Ireland, Eire)	Mar 1 – Oct 31
Hinds/does (Scotland)	Feb 16 – Oct 20

Roe deer bucks (England, Wales)	Nov 1 – Mar 31
Roe deer bucks (Scotland)	Oct 21 – Mar 31
Roe deer does (England, Wales)	Mar 1 – Oct 31
Roe deer does (Scotland)	Apr 1 – Oct 20

NOTES

1   The close seasons for red deer, fallow deer and sika deer are the same.

2   There is no close season for the muntjac or the Chinese water deer.

Bibliography

Brander, M. (1986) *Deer Stalking in Britain*, The Sportsman's Press

British Association for Shooting and Conservation (1984) *Handbook of Shooting*, BASC

British Association for Shooting and Conservation (1989) *The New Wildfowler*, Stanley Paul

Chaplin, R. E. (1977) *Deer*, Blandford Press

Douglas, J. (1983) *The Sporting Gun*, David & Charles

Lawrence, M. J. and Brown, R. W. (1974) *Mammals of Britain: Their Tracks, Trails and Signs*, Blandford Press

Martin, B. P. (1984) *Sporting Birds of the British Isles*, David & Charles

Nahlik, A. J. (1987) *Wild Deer: Their Culling, Conservation and Management*, Ashford Press

Ogilvie, M. A. (1978) *Wild Geese*, T. & A.D. Poyser

Reader's Digest Association (1969) *Book of British Birds*, Drive Publications

Whitehead, G. K. (1972) *Deer of the World*, Constable

Whitehead, G. K. (1982) *Hunting and Stalking Deer Throughout the World*, Batsford

Whitehead, G. K. (1986) *Practical Deer Stalking*, Constable

Index